To George Talbot Goodspeed, A.B. '25
who can tell a good oath from a bad one

T0338893

FIRST IMPRESSIONS

Printing in Cambridge, 1639–1989

HUGH AMORY

An exhibition at the Houghton Library
and at the Harvard Law School Library
October 6 through October 27, 1989

Harvard University
Cambridge, Massachusetts

Donors

ENGLISH TITLES

1. William Bentinck-Smith, 1968
   Daniel B. Fearing, 1915
   James B. Munn, 1932
   Penelope B. Noyes
   Bertha L. Teel, 1986
2. Mrs. E.D. Brandegee, 1908
   William Davis, 1912
   Frederick L. Gay, 1916
   Samuel Savage, 1766
   Isaac Smith, 1765
3. Frederick L. Gay, 1916
   Nathaniel C. Leeds, 1866
   Charles E. Norton, 1905
4. Middlecott Cooke, 1764
   Mr. and Mrs. Kenneth Murdoch, 1974
   The New England Society, 1912
5. J.J. Cooke, 1883
   Michael R. Gannett, 1982
   Ernest L. Gay, 1927
   Rebecca Holbrook, 1794
6. William H. Claflin, 1971
   Alfred Mitchell, 1908
   A.B. Valentine, 1875

INDIAN PRINTING

7. Friends of the Library, 1941
   Mrs. James M. Hunnewell, 1967
   Charles E. Norton, 1905
   William Prescott, 1845
   Israel Thorndike, 1818
8. Helen J. Dubbs, 1981
   Ernest L. Gay, 1927
   Philip Hofer, 1984
   William I. Morse, 1945
   John Quinan, 1870
9. Alfred Bowditch, 1913
   Middlecott Cooke, 1764
   Frederick L. Gay, 1916
   Paul Grinke, 1985
   Elizabeth P. Sever, 1855
10. Jonathan Fox, 1765
    Harrison D. Horblit, 1953
    Harold Murdock, 1935
    Joseph T. Tower, 1933

LEGAL ISSUES

1. Friends of the Library, 1941
   Frederick L. Gay, 1916
   A.A. Houghton, Jr., 1940
2. Middlecott Cooke, 1764
   A.R. Pope, 1846
   John Usher, ca. 1675
3. Middlecott Cooke, 1764
   The Misses Ellis, 1928
   Massachusetts Historical Society, 1935
4. F.S. Ferguson, 1953
   Philip Hofer, 1942
   Bertha L. Teel, 1986
5. Friends of the Library, 1967
   Mr. & Mrs. Kenneth N. Hill, 1981
   James L. Hook, 1934
   Charles E. Norton, 1905
   Stephen W. Phillips, 1940
   John Salkeld, 1899
6. Frederick L. Gay, 1916
   Benjamin Lincoln, before 1800
   Joseph Story, 1837
   West Publishing Company, 1955

Lenders

American Antiquarian Society
Hugh Amory
Arnold Arboretum, Harvard University
Harvard University Archives
Massachusetts Historical Society
Peabody Museum, Harvard University
Roxbury Latin School
United Church Board for World Ministries

Purchases

Duplicate Fund
Lee M. Friedman Memorial Fund
George Schünemann Jackson Fund
George Shepard Lee Fund
George L. Lincoln Fund
Andrew Preston Peabody Fund
John Harvey Treat Fund
Grant Walker Fund
Charles Warren Fund

Copyright © 1989 by the President and Fellows of Harvard College
Designed by Richard C. Bartlett

INTRODUCTION

We customarily distinguish the technology of printing from the social and economic organization (publishing) that supports it, and again from alternative technologies of tongue and pen (authorship) that compete with it. These are useful distinctions, though their boundaries are fluid, and it is easy to overlook or underestimate the complex reality they define for the existence of a text. Bibliography is the study of textual environments, a kind of ecology, which goes far beyond the physical embodiment of a text on the page, or even readership. After the first five years of their existence, relatively few books are read at all; some, like Shakespeare or the Bible, are normally encountered at second hand; some are fabulous reports of uncertain texts and editions. Printing in Cambridge involves an understanding of all these locations and habitats.

I have divided the exhibition into three complementary sections. "English Titles" covers by far the most numerous and intellectually varied productions of the first press, which, however, required a comparatively limited outlay of labor and capital. "Indian Printing" accounted for the overwhelming bulk of the paper that passed through the press; few titles, for a strictly local market. And finally, I deal in "Legal Issues" with a pathological case: few of the lawyers' tools were actually printed in America, but these include one of the few seventeenth-century books whose American-printed sheets were actually reissued in England. The first two sections are exhibited in Houghton Library, the last in the Harvard Law School Treasure Room.

Each section focuses on a single book: the Bay Psalm Book; the Eliot Indian Bible; and *The Laws and Liberties* of Massachusetts. These three books have become pure icons, which can only be reproduced in facsimile, and which are not only unread and unexamined, but, in the case of the Bible, in a dead language. A textual and bibliographical reexamination of thse idols is long overdue. The bibliography of the Bible, in particular, is crippled by the myth of Apostle John Eliot, translating from Hebrew to Massachusett, and by a tradition of bibliophily that has turned an Indian monument into a white man's treasure.

At the end of every section I append a brief essay: a fresh census of the Bay Psalm Book, showing how the eleven extant copies came out of hiding and when; biographies of James Printer, the first and last man who could read Massachusett in the composing stick, and of Job Nesutan, co-author of the "Eliot Indian Bible"; and an edition of the Day-Green accounts, heretofore available only in filiopietistic type-facsimile, quasi-facsimile transcript, or facsimile.

Fifty years ago, Samuel Eliot Morison called for a list of books that were in America before 1700. The superiority of such a tool for historical inquiry over either Evans or Sabin ought to be obvious, but isn't. We continue to assess book production by "Evans numbers," glibly equating a single half-sheet with an entire Bible. With Evans, too, we confine American books to American printing. For the other part of the colonial elephant (taking Evans as the tail in this parable of the blind men) one must grope about the vast gray body of Wing. In short, the historian who wants a reliable record of what seventeenth-century Americans wrote and read has no very solid reference work. This exhibition can only hint at these broader issues, and, in a very small way, show specimen *sondages*. For the future, one may look forward to the new edition of the 1796 catalogue of the Library of the Massachusetts Historical Society, now in preparation.

This is an exhibition that is deeply indebted to the kindness of friends and strangers. Colleagues at Houghton Library, the Harvard University Archives, the Harvard Law School Treasure Room, and the Massachusetts Historical Society have pursued many more books and manuscripts than I was able to exhibit, and suggested some I would never have thought of exhibiting, but did. In particular, I must thank Roger Stoddard for inspiration and expert support, as always; Michael Winship, who has endured unsatiated many false leads and idiotic drafts of parts of this catalogue; and Kitzi Pantzer, for more information

on English printers than I rightly know what to do with. Professor John Hewson and Wilfrid Prosper kindly deciphered our Micmac MS., and Professor George F. Aubin explained things Indian and alleviated the terrors of Massachusett. John Alden sent me a xerox of his unpublished, important paper on the Prince Library, much of it formerly in his care. I am especially grateful for the photographic skills of Vic Santamaria, Dan Sullivan, and Rick Stafford.

The exhibition catalogue is dedicated to a great friend of Harvard University Library. To mention only top billings on our subject, he steered the *Capitall lawes* from Lincoln Cathedral and the Cambridge *Platform* from the Streeter Sale to new, right homes; and in the recent episode of a forged Freeman's Oath, his faith in provenance, against a formidable array of physical evidence and "expert" opinion, was thoroughly vindicated. Where books come from, not just what they are, continues to matter to us.

This catalogue has been made possible by the generosity of Michael Zinman, Charles J. Tanenbaum, Frank S. Streeter and Henry S. Streeter.

HUGH AMORY

.j5.

Der Schrifftgiesser.

Ich geuß die Schrifft zu der Druckrey
Gemacht auß Wißmat/Zin vnd Bley/
Die kan ich auch gerecht justiern/
Die Buchstaben zusammn ordniern
Lateinisch vnd Teutscher Geschrifft
Was auch die Griechisch Sprach antrifft
Mit Versalen/ Puncten vnd Zügn
Daß sie zu der Truckrey sich fügen.
              E iij   Der

Jost Amman, "Der Schrifftgiesser"

IESVS CHRISTVS
SVMMVS MAGISTER
CÆLESTIS DOCTRINÆ
AVCTOR.

S. SILVESTER CHRISTI DOMINI VICARIVS.	A ET Ω	CONSTANTINVS IMPERATOR ECCL. DEFENSOR.

ADAM
Diuinitus edoctus, primus scientiarum & litterarum inuentor.

f	gh	ſ	n	m	l	k	i	t	hh	z	u	h	d	g	b	a

th	ſc	r	q	zz

MOYSES
Antiquas Hebraicas litteras inuenit.

f	gh	ſ	n	m	l	k	i	t	hh	z	u	h	d	g	b	a

th	ſc	r	q	zz

ABRAHAM
Syras, & Chaldaicas litteras inuenit.

i	t	hh	z	u	h	d	g	b	a

th	ſc	r	q	zz	f	gh	ſ	n	m	l	c

ESDRAS
Nouas Hebræorum litteras inuenit.

c	i	t	ch	z	u	h	d	g	b	a
t.th	ſ	ſc	r	k	ts	p.ph	gh	ſ	n	m	l

Arabici Characteres.

ſſ	ſc	ſ	z	r	dh	d	ch	h	g	th	t	b	a

i	l	a	u	h	n	m	l	q	ch	f	gh	hh	thd	tt	dh

PHOENIX
Litteras Phœnicibus tradidit.

ſ	n	m	l	c	i	t	th	hh	z	u	h	d	g	b	a

th	ſc	r	q	ſſ	f	gh

S. IO. CHRYSOSTOMVS
Litterarum Armenicarum Auctor.

a.	p.b	c.g.	d.t.	e.ie.	z.	æ.e.	be.	th.	g.h.x.	i.	l.	hh.	kk.tz.zz.

c.g.κ.q.	h.	ſſ.ts.x.	gl.l.	gh.	m.	i.	n.	ſ.ſc.o.	ſz.	p.b.	q.z.	rr.rh.	ſ.

u.	td.	r.	zz.	y.	p.pſ.	sh.	cu.	pz.	o.

S. HIERONYMVS
Litterarum Illyricarum inuentor.

a	b	u	gh	d	e	ſg	ſz	ſz	is	i	gi	ju	κ	l

m	n	o	p	r	ſ	t	u	f	h	pſ	cc	z	od	ſc	I	ia	iu

S. CYRILLVS
Aliarum Illyricarum litterarum Auctor.

А	Б	Г	Д	Е	Ж	З	З	Н	Ѳ	I	К	Л	М	Н	О
a	b	g	d	e	x	ſ	z	i	thi	i	κl	l	m	n	o

п	р	с	т	ȣ	ф	Ꚇ	ψ	ѡ	ц	ч	ш	щ	✥
p	r	ſ	t	u	f	ch	pſ	o	z	cc	ſc	x	ſct

LINVS THEBANVS
Litterarum Græcarum inuentor.

А	Б	Г	Δ	Е	I	К	Λ	М	N
a	b	g	d	e	i	κ	l	m	n

Ξ	О	Π	Ρ	Σ	Т
x	o	p	r	ſ	t

CADMVS PHOENICIS FRATER
Litteras haſce in Græciam intulit.

А	Б	Г	Δ	Е	I	К	Λ	М	N	Ξ
a	b	g	d	e	i	κ	l	m	n	x

О	Π	Ρ	Σ	Φ
o	p	r	ſ	ph

CECROPS DIPHYES
Primus Atheniensium Rex, Græcarum litterarum inuentor.

А	Б	Г	Δ	Е	I	К	Λ	М	N	Ξ
a	b	g	d	e	i	κ	l	m	n	x

О	Π	Ρ	Σ	Т	Φ
o	p	r	ſ	t	ph

PYTHAGORAS
Y. litteram ad humanæ vitæ exemplum inuenit.

$$Y$$

SIMONIDES MELICVS
Quattuor Græcarum litterarum inuentor.

Z.	H.	Ψ.	Ω.
z	i	pſ	o

EPICHARMVS SICVLVS
Duas Græcas addidit litteras.

Θ.	Χ.
th	ch

PALAMEDES
Bello Troiano Græcis litteras quattuor adiecit.

Θ.	Ξ.	Φ.	Χ.
th	x	ph	ch

EVANDER CARMENTAE F.
Aborigines litteras docuit.

H.	K.	Q.	X.	Y.	Z.

NICOSTRATA CARMENTA
Latinarum litterarum inuentrix.

A.	B.	C.	D.	E.	G.	H.	I.	L.
M.	**N.**	**O.**	**P.**	**R.**	**S.**	**T.**	**V.**	

ANGELO ROCCA
Variarum linguarum alphabeta (detail)

I. ENGLISH TITLES

1. Print and Privilege

The incorporation of the Stationers' Company in 1557 effectively limited printing in England to London and the two Universities. In 1603, the Company began to acquire monopolies in certain valuable texts, later known as the "English stock": psalms, almanacs, and prayer books among them. These privileges were further strengthened in 1637 by a Star Chamber decree. The Rev. Josse Glover's plans for printing in New England were realized within this framework of prohibitions.

New England itself was little affected by English law at first, but print and privilege arrived on these shores together. The General Court opposed the establishment of a second press before 1675, and printing did not really begin to proliferate before the lapse of the Licensing Act, in 1695. London privilege could have had little impact on the Cambridge press before it acquired a London market in the 1670's; but as this commercial nexus tightened, the New Englanders gradually abandoned their version of the psalms for Tate and Brady's, belonging to the Stationers' Company. Tate and Brady's was better poetry, they said—as though the issue were aesthetic.

ANGELO ROCCA *Variarvm linguarvm alphabeta et inventores* Romae : D. Basa, 1595.
Typefounding initially spread with printing, but by 1500 began to contract to a few centers; the type specimen is a device for connecting dispersed presses and concentrated founders.

HANS SACHS *Eygentliche Beschreibung aller Stände auff Erden* Franckfurt am Mayn : G. Raben for S. Feyerabend, 1568.
"Der Schrifftgiesser," by Jost Amman.

GEORG HOFMANN & GEORG WOLFFGER *New-auffgesetztes Format-Büchlein* Gratz : Widmannstetterische Druckerei, [1670?]
The so-called "single lay of the case"; the Cambridge press was using a double lay by 1663, but may have used this more primitive arrangement for the Bay Psalm Book.

ENGLAND AND WALES. COURT OF STAR CHAMBER *A decree of Starre-Chamber concerning printing* London : R. Barker and the assigns of J. Bill, 1637.
Restricting typefounding to four persons in London and forbidding the sale or importation of type without official sanction.

GEORGE WITHER *The psalmes of David* [Amsterdam?] : C. Gerrits van Breugel, 1632.
Opposition from the Stationers' Company prevented Wither from publishing his translation in England.

MASSACHUSETTS (Colony) GENERAL COURT *Order*, 2 June 1663.
Setting the Cambridge press at liberty, pending the appointment of new licensers.

STEVEN DAY *Indenture*, 7 June 1638.
Indentured as a locksmith, Day nevertheless managed to run the printing press for Elizabeth Glover, until her death in 1643.
Lent by the Harvard University Archives.

SEVENTEENTH-CENTURY TYPE from the site of the Indian College, Harvard Yard, found in 1979.
The sorts include a cross formée (✠), used to denote the points in the liturgy where the

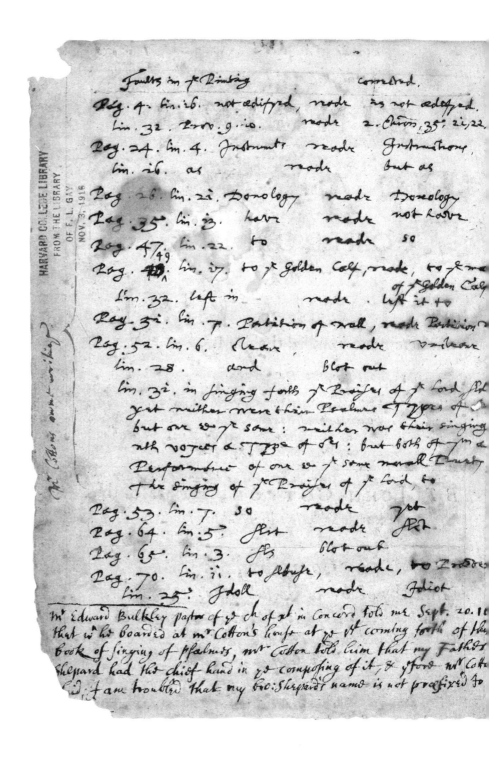

priest should make the sign of the cross. No impression of this sort has been found in an American book before 1800, though a pica cross formée does appear.

Lent by the Peabody Museum.

2. *"Singing of psalms a Gospel-ordinance"*

Nineteenth-century New Englanders invented the name of the "Bay Psalm Book" to denote — without actually saying so — the version decreed and sung within Massachusetts Bay Colony — not in Plymouth, not in Salem (Naumkeag) — before the charter of 1691 abolished the Colony's independence. None of these implications have a demonstrable basis in fact: no synod resolved to make the version; any congregation was free to reject

OF THE
SINGING
OF *PSALMES.*

CHAPTER. I.
Propounding the severall Questions about it; and Handling the First.

O prevent the godly-minded from making melody to the Lord in Singing his Praises with one accord (I meane with one heart, and one voyce) Satan hath mightily bestirred himselfe, to breed a discord in the hearts of some, by filling their heads with foure heads of scruples about the Duty.

1. *Touching the Duty it selfe of singing Psalmes with lively voyce,* whether there be any such worship at all now to be allowed and practised in the dayes of the New Testament?

2. *Touching the matter to be sung,* whether Scripture *Psalmes* penned by *David, Asaph, Moses, Solomon, Hezekiah, Habakkuk, Zachary, Simeon, Deborah, Mary, Elizabeth,* or the like: *Or songs immediately indited by some personall spirituall gift of some Officer, or Member of the Church ?*

3. *Touching the Singers ,* If vocall singing may be allowed.

Who must Sing ? { 1. Whether one for all the rest, the rest onely saying Amen ? or the whole Congregation?
2. Whether women as well as men, or men alone ?
3. Whether carnall men and Pagans, as well as Church-members and Christians ?

B   4. *Touching*

JOHN COTTON *Singing of psalmes a Gospel-ordinance*

it; and Presbyterians as well as Congregationalists sang it, in England and Scotland as well as in America.

The main ideologue of the new version, John Cotton, shows no interest in liturgical uniformity, and the version itself, where it differs from the received Anglican metrical version by Sternhold and Hopkins, generally conforms to King James's Bible. Strictly speaking, it is not a paraphrase at all, since it distinguishes the original words (in roman) from the infrequent additions of the translators (in italic), and even represents Hebrew morphology by hyphenations (as in Ainsworth). For liturgical authority Cotton appealed to I Cor. xiv:15–16 and the practice of the church in Caesarea under Saint Basil the Great. Without external evidence, it would be hard to show the connection of the text to Massachusetts Bay Colony or even with Congregationalism.

SAINT BASIL the Great *Works (Latin & Greek)* Parisiis : C. Sonnius, 1637–1638.
Cited by Cotton as authority for "lining out a psalm" to the congregation.

DAVID PAREUS *Opera theologica exegetica* [Frankfurt a.M.] : J. Roos's widow, 1647.
President Leverett's copy; Cotton cites the first edition of Pareus's commentary on I
Corinthians (1614)—of which I can locate only the BN copy—to show that Psalms were
ordained to be sung, as well as read and preached.

JOHANN BUXTORF *Thesaurus grammatica linguae sanctae Hebraeae*, Ed. 4ta.
Basileae : L. König, 1629.
Cited by Cotton to show that the Psalms were in meter; John Harvard owned a copy of
this edition.

BIBLE (Authorized Version) *The Holy Bible* London : R. Barker and assignes of J.
Bill, 1637 [i.e. 1638].
Roman for the original tongues; italic for the vernacular additions; small capitals for the
ineffable name of God.

HENRY AINSWORTH *The Book of Psalmes* Amsterdam : G. Thorpe, 1612.
Mentioned in the Bay Psalm Book for the "difficulty" of his tunes.

JOHN COTTON *Singing of psalmes a Gospel-ordinance* London : M. S[immons]. for H.
Allen and J. Rothwell, 1647.
The author's copy; presented to Thomas Shepard, with his MS corrections.

3. William Jones and John Norton's types

The ill-sorted mixture of type in the Bay Psalm Book argues that the type was already
used when Glover got it. William Jones (d. 1643) is the likeliest source for the exotic
fonts, and perhaps persuaded John Norton to supply the roman and italic. Jones was a
Puritan sympathizer who had printed works by the colonists John Cotton, John White and
William Wood, as well as by the Puritan Hebraist Hugh Broughton (satirized by Ben
Jonson as "Zeal-of-the-Land Busy"). Jones had a history of trouble with the Star Chamber,
who forced him to cede his business to his partner Thomas Paine in 1637. The sale of
type and perhaps of ironwork for the Cambridge press presumably took place about this
date.

Only two works survive that were certainly printed from this supply, which included
pica and long primer roman and italic as well as the 95 english used for the text. At some
early date, a fresh supply of type was obtained, perhaps the pica used in the 1648 *Laws*
and the Cambridge *Platform*. The Cambridge Press continued to use the english hebrews
and greeks, but abandoned the romans and italics after printing the Bay Psalm Book and
the 1643 Harvard *Theses*.

HARVARD COLLEGE *Theses (1643)* Cantabrigiae : [S. Day], mens. 8 1643.
115 great primer greek; the size is concealed by the blank space above.
Lent by the Massachusetts Historical Society.

JOHN DAVENPORT *A discourse about civil government in a new plantation whose
design is religion* Cambridge : S. Green and M. Johnson, 1663.
115 great primer greek and 85 pica roman and italic.

WILLIAM ALABASTER *Spiraculum tubarum* London : W. Jones, [1633]
95 unpointed english hebrew.

LITERA
כ CAPH.

כבב Inde כּוֹכָב,Chald:כּוֹכַב,Syr.כַּוְכַב, Arab.כּוֹכָב kcukeb *stella*, quæ nunquã כָּבָה *extinguitur*.
Rabb: כָּבָב *cacabus, olla*.

כבר Inde כִּבֵּר, Chald: כִּבֵּר Syr:כַּבְּר *orbis*. Tria autem significat. 1. *locum planum et depressum, ac germinibus præditum*, ac convenit cum כַּר *pratum*. 2. *panem, in tortæ formam coactum, placentam*. 3. *metallum*.

כָּאַב Duo significat. I. כָּאַב, Chald: כָּאַב, Syr. כְּאֵב, Arab. כּאב *cib doluit corpore vel animo, infirmus, tristis fuit*.

Nom. מִכְאַב & כְּאֵב, Chald. כֵּיב, & כַּב,Syr: כְּאַב, Arab.כּאאבה *dolor, morbus, perturbatio animi, cruciatus, affectus molestus*.

Chald. כָּאַב, Arab:כּיב *dolens, ægrotus, tristis.* הַכְיָאִית *cum dolore, anxiè, instanter*.

Arab: אכְתִיב *mæstus fuit.* *contristatus*.

II. הִכְאִיב & כָּאַב per metaphoram, *corcorruptus est, corrupit*.

כָּאָה Duo significat. I. כָּאֵר.Inde Niph. נִכְאָה *turbatus, perturbatus, tristis, contristatus, consternatus fuit*.

Nom. כָּאִים, est חֵיל כְּלָאִים *turba tristium, afflictorum, pauperum*.

II. Syr.כָּאָא *molestus fuit, objurgavit, increpavit, inhibuit*.

כאר כָּאַר, *fodit, perfodit.*

כבב Arabicè בְּרָאב *frusta rotunda.* אֶכְבָּאָה & כבאבא *inclinatio capitis.* כְּהִבְבּוּא *capite subverso dejicientur.* מַכְבּוּב *cooperiens.* אִכְרָאב *opertio.*

כבד Tria significat. I. כָּבֵר, Chal. *gravis fuit quantitate aut qualitate, magnitudine vel multitudine, pondere vel numero, divitijs, honore, gloria*.
Nom: כָּבֵר *gravis, numerosus, multus, dives, honorabilis.* כָּבֵר *idem.*
Subst: כָּבוֹד *gravitas, honor, gloria, dignitas, majestas, claritas, divitiæ, honorarium, donum, præmium*.

כְּבֵרוּת, & כְּבוּדָּה, & כָּבֵר *gravitas, onus, multitudo, gloria.*
II. Deinde כָּבֵר, Chald:כָּבֵר, Arab:כְּבֵר *kebd epar, jecur.* מכבוד *makbud hepaticus.*
III. Rabb. מְכַבֵּר verrit, הִכְבִּיר *scopæ.* כַּבָה *extinctus fuit.* Rabb:כבּוּ *extinctio.* Inde כֶּבֵל, Chald. כְּבַר *compes, catena.*

Rabb: כָּבוֹל & כְּבֵל *annulus*, qui de collo servi suspenditur.
Verb.Rabb. כָּבַל, Chald. כְּבַר *ligavit, constrinxit nervo aut compede*. כְּבִיל *ligatus, constrictus, compeditus.* Arab: כְּבַל *cabal fibula, spinter.*
Inde Syr: Piel כַּבֵּן: & Hiphil אכְבּן *texit, operuit, induit, pellibus cinxit.* מְכַבֵּן & כְּבִין *tectus, opertus.* מַכְבְּנָא *capitis ornamentum.*
Chald. כְּבִינָא *vestis subtilis* ἱμάτιον, *sindon*.
Rabb. כָּבֵן *operimentum agnorum.*

כבס Inde Piel כִּבֵּס *lavit, purgavit, abluit, eluit, candidavit.*
Nomen כּוֹבֵס *fullo.*
Rabb:כּוֹבֶסֶת *ramus palmæ.*
Arab. כָּאבוס et כָּבוּס *incubus.*

כבע Inde כָּבַע,idem quod קוֹבַע, *galera, galerus, cassis.*
Rabb: כּוֹבַעַת *capita spicarum.*
Arabicè כבע *cuba galerita, cassita.* קבאן *alauda.*
Rabb. כָּבֵץ *incubus.*

כבר Arab. כבר *cabar magnus fuit quantitate continua et discreta, grandis, multus, creber, copiosus fuit.* Arab. *granduit, ingranduit, crevit, superbivit.* Arab. אתכבר et אסתכבר *superbijt, elatus, inflatus fuit.*
Nom: כַּבִּיר, et כָּאַבִּיר *abundante,* Arab. כביר *kabir, et* כאבר *magnus, summus, grandis, multus, copiosus.* כְּבִיר *pulvinar hispidum.* כְּבָרָה *cribrum.* מַכְבֵּר *stragula.*

מכבר

Moses Capell   *Gods valvation of mans soule*   London : W. J[ones]. for N. Bourne, 1632.
> 95 english roman and italic, with 115 great primer greek; from the Mather Library.

New Testament   *Hē Kainē Diathēkē*   Cantabrigiae : T. Buck, 1632.
> 115 Great primer greek, borrowed from Oxford University Press. From the libraries of Cotton and Nathanael Mather.

Edward Brerewood   *Enquiries touching the diversity of languages, and religions, through the chiefe parts of the world*   London : J. Norton for Joyce Norton and R. Whitaker, 1635.
> 95 English roman and italic.

Stanley Morison   *John Fell, the University Press, and the 'Fell' types*   Oxford : Clarendon Press, 1967.
> This specimen is printed from the original types.

John Cotton   *Gods promise to his plantations*   London : W. Jones for J. Bellamy, 1634.

4. The Whole Book of Psalms

The 1700 copies of the first edition of the Bay Psalm Book and the 2000 copies of the second edition must have saturated the Massachusetts market, which amounted to only 13,000 souls in 1640, rising to 90,000 at the end of the century. Not surprisingly, later seventeenth-century editions were mostly printed abroad. Richard Chiswell starts a regular sequence of London editions in 1671, which perhaps found a vent in New England as well down to 1695, when a regular sequence of American editions begins.

Translated by Richard Mather, John Eliot, and other "chief Divines in the Country"; edited, with a preface, by John Cotton, the Bay Psalm Book has become a symbol of Congregational worship. The only modern reprints are in facsimile and represent the version and title that was least widely dispersed. Thomas Prince was the last person to examine the text with any care, and entered his collation of the first two editions in the margin of a Boston Library copy (whited out in facsimile). Even the facsimiles show unrecorded press variants in the first edition—evidence, if any were needed, that no one has ever compared copies. Evidently the book has become iconic and critics are content to reenact the prototypographical moment without examining its significance.

Bay Psalm Book   *The whole booke of psalmes*   New York : New England Society, [1911]
> A photofacsimile (often retouched) of the Huntington Library copy.

Psalms (Sternhold-Hopkins Version)   *The whole book of psalmes*   [Cambridge] : T. Buck and R. Daniel, 1638.
> The Bay Psalm Book uses the same tunes, title and even epigrams as the Sternhold-Hopkins version. In this copy of the Sternhold-Hopkins version, a child has drawn a piratical portrait of his tutor (pasted over, but retraced in pencil (by a later childish owner?))

Bay Psalm Book   *The whole booke of psalmes*   [Cambridge : S. Day], 1640.

BAY PSALM BOOK   *A literal reprint of the Bay Psalm Book*   Cambridge : Riverside Press, for C. B. Richardson, 1862.
The Riverside Press type facsimile of the John Carter Brown Library copy is noteworthy for its amazing ability to reproduce in metal all the typographical flaws of the original; note the press variants (which are not typos).
Lent by the Massachusetts Historical Society.

BAY PSALM BOOK   *The whole booke of psalmes*   [Chicago] : University of Chicago Press, [1956]
A composite photofacsimile of the Prince Collection copies in the Boston Public Library.

PSALMS (Sternhold-Hopkins Version)   *The whole booke of psalmes*   London : J. Day, 1562.
Though printed in black-letter, this provides the layout for the Bay Psalm Book. There were no roman single-column versions printed before 1640.

5. *Writing*

The texts that never reached print in seventeenth-century New England are as intriguing as those that did; sometimes MS. copies have survived in greater numbers than many printed books. Over twenty copies of the Harvard College laws known as admittaturs survive. The students also copied some text-books, such as Charles Morton's *Compendium of physics* (I have noted some fifteen copies in Boston libraries); the earliest American-printed texts are William Brattle's *Compendium logicae* and Judah Monis' Hebrew grammar, both in 1735. The students complained particularly about the hardship of copying the latter. Finally, a wide range of legal and commercial documents were multiplied in MS., which required penmanship, a skill taught separately from writing. Houghton has a collection of some 135 prize examples by students of various ages, written in the school of Abiah Holman.

Nevv Englands first fruits   London : R. O[verton]. and G. D[exter]. for Henry Overton, 1643.
The first printing of the 1642 College laws; the laws were not printed again until 1790.

HARVARD COLLEGE   *The lawes and orders of Harvard College* (1655)
The official copy, in English and Latin. The 1655 and 1734 laws provide that the candidate must copy them, to be admitted. Presumably the college hoped that they would be better embedded in undergraduates' memory by this device; but the surviving copies are highly inaccurate (though certified by the president and the candidate's tutor).
Lent by the Harvard University Archives.

HARVARD COLLEGE   *Admittaturs:* Jonathan Mitchell, 22 Oct. 1683; Joseph Belcher, 13 Jun. 1686; Warham Williams, 19 Oct. 1715.
Mitchell admittatur lent by the Massachusetts Historical Society; Williams admittatur lent by Harvard University Archives.

CHARLES MORTON   *Compendium of physics,* copied by Obadiah Ayers (A.B. 1710); ditto, copied by Samuel Dunbar (A.B. 1721).
Though this was used as a Harvard textbook from 1687 to at least 1723, it was never printed.
Lent by Harvard University Archives.

Mather ~~Mathew Whitington his Book~~ November 1. 1735.

דִּקְדּוּק

לָשׁוֹן עִבְרִית

DICKDOOK LESHON GNEBREET.

A

GRAMMAR

OF THE

Hebrew Tongue,

BEING

An ESSAY

To bring the Hebrew Grammar into English,
to Facilitate the

INSTRUCTION

Of all those who are desirous of acquiring a clear Idea of this

Primitive Tongue

by their own Studies ;

In order to their more distinct Acquaintance with the SACRED ORACLES of
the Old Testament, according to the Original. And
Published more especially for the Use of the STUDENTS of *HARVARD-COLLEGE*
at *Cambridge*, in NEW-ENGLAND.

נֶחְבַּר וְהוּחֲת בְּעִיוּן נִמְרָץ עַל יְדֵי
יְהוּדָה מוֹנִישׁ

Composed and accurately Corrected,

By JUDAH MONIS, *M. A.*

BOSTON, N.E.

Printed by JONAS GREEN, and are to be Sold by the AUTHOR
at his House in *Cambridge.* MDCCXXXV.

Novemb. 1735

O Lord

Johannes Tucker

John

Judah Monis Grammer Now possesd by J. Tucke & possessed possesd

Almss

Almsbury

December

Boston New England IIII N 14 1735

Cambridge College

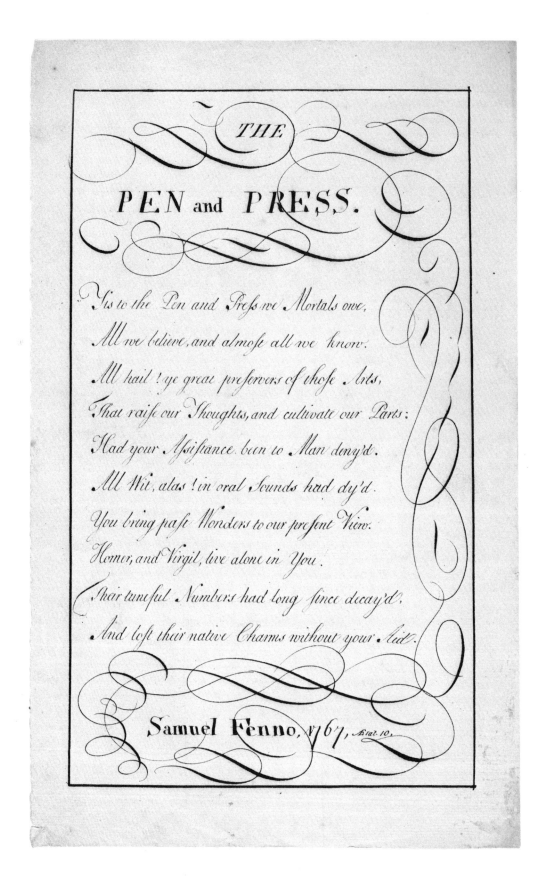

JUDAH MONIS *Dikduk leshon ʿIvrit* Boston: J. Green, 1735.
John Tucker (A.B. 1741) and other undergraduates display their penmanship in the margins and the fly-leaf.

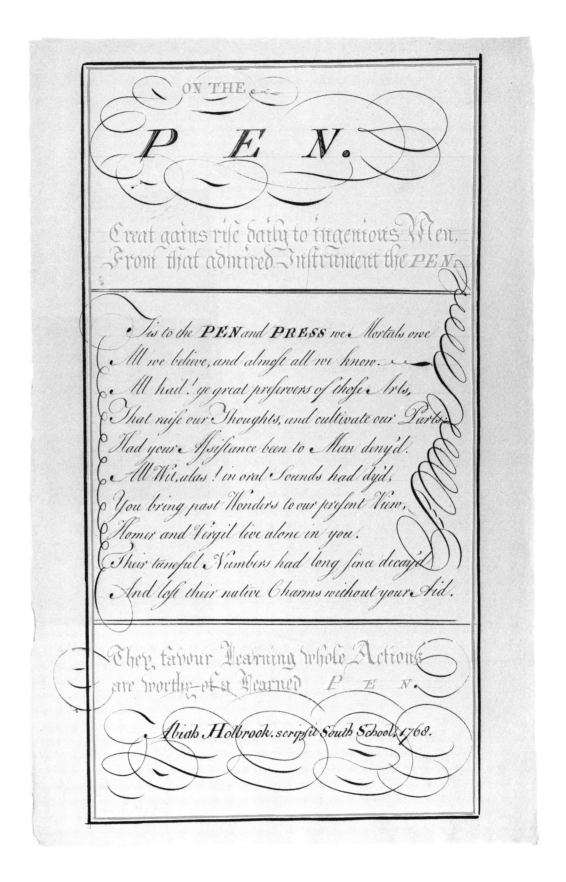

SAMUEL FENNO (age 10)   *The pen and press*, 1767; and ABIAH HOLBROOK *On the pen*, 1768.

These copies come from South School, Boston, where Abiah Holbrook's father taught penmanship.

6. Culture to Commerce

Apart from the Bay Psalm Book, most seventeenth-century New England English titles had a limited market: almanacs for the meridian of Boston and Cambridge, Harvard College programs, funeral elegies, and a slew of personally conceived catechisms. The first American-printed book to be regularly sold in England is Richard Chiswell's reissue of the 1672 Massachusetts Laws (1675). This is the first symptom of something we might call a "book trade"—i.e. the exchange of American for English sheets. Beaver skins, salt cod and barrel staves for books are something else. A study of the provenance of American books in European libraries might be very revealing.

Not by coincidence, the 1670's saw the establishment of a second press in Boston, the first printed illustrations, and publications like Hubbard's *Narrative* that aim at informing a wider audience than Boston. Earlier equivalents, like Wood's *Prospect*, had been printed in England. Hezekiah Usher imports psalms and Bibles printed in the Netherlands.

STEVEN DAY & SAMUEL GREEN *MS memoranda of revenues from the press*, [26 Nov. 1655]
> Lent by Harvard University Archives.

HARVARD COLLEGE *Steward's Accounts*, 1650–1663.
> Gershom Bulkeley buys a Bay Psalm Book (1651) from the printer Samuel Green; together with an almanac and a haircut, for 3/0.
> Lent by Harvard University Archives.

CAMBRIDGE SYNOD (1648) *A platform of church discipline gathered out of the Word of God* London : W. Bentley for J. Ridley, 1652.
> After two experimental codes by John Cotton and Nathaniel Ward, the Colony enacted separate laws for Church and State in 1648. The political franchise, however, continued to hinge on church membership, a condition that is sometimes called "democracy," because it gave the vote to Lazarus, or "theocracy," because it excluded certain rich men. Lazarus finally lost the battle with the Province Charter (1691).
> The Church code was reprinted in England, in this highly incorrect edition, which had to be suppressed; only three copies survive. Harvard also has a copy of the first edition.

WILLIAM HUBBARD *A narrative of the troubles with the Indians in New-England* Boston : J. Foster, 1677.
> The official account of King Philip's War, a confederacy of the "United Colonies" of Massachusetts, Plymouth and Connecticut against the Wampanoags under King Philip, the Narragansetts and heterodox Rhode Island; excusing Puritan aggression as a defense against barbarism.

INCREASE MATHER *The life and death of that reverend man of God Mr. Richard Mather* Cambridge : S. G[reen]. and M. J[ohnson]., 1670.
> The frontispiece portrait of Richard Mather by John Foster was printed ca. 1675.
> The portrait and the map are the typical forms of Puritan art, which avoids representing the unnamed. The Mathers even excised the printers' marks from books in their library, presumably because they were not part of "the word."

JOHN FOSTER, *Richard Mather:* in *Biblia Hebraica* Antverpiae : C. Plantin, 1584.
> From the library of Increase Mather, with the Foster portrait mounted on the front cover. In this state, the lower block has been planed down, probably to remove the impressions of Aries and Cancer. The black parts became larger and the white parts shrank.

THOMAS VINCENT *Gods terrible voice in the city of London* Cambridge : S. Green, 1667 [i.e. 1668].

In 1668, the General Court summoned Samuel Green and Marmaduke Johnson "to give an account of what bookes haue lately been printed at Cambridge." They acknowledged fourteen titles, all but one first published in England—a sharp break with their previous publications, which were almost exclusively confined to colonial properties.

These new titles may be identified as *A choice drop of honey from the Rock Christ* / Thomas Wilcox [1st ed. not recorded]; *Precepts for Christian practice* [abridged] / Edward Reyner (1668); *The way to a blessed estate* / Ezekiel Culverwell [1st ed. 1622]; "The Assembly of Divines Chatchise," probably an abridgement; *Gods terrible voice in the city of London* / Thomas Vincent (1667 [1668]); *Tydings from Rome* / John Flavel (1668); *Eye-salve for England* / Evan Price [1st ed. 1667]; and *The young mans monitor* [abridged?] / Samuel Crossman [1st ed. 1664], all by Green—and by Johnson, "the primer" ; "ye psalter"; *Daily meditations* / Philip Pain (1668); *The rise, spring and foundation of the Anabaptists* / adapted by J. Scottow from the French of G. de Brès (1668); *The isle of pines* / Henry Neville [1st ed. 1668?]; and *The righteous mans evidence of heaven* / Timothy Rogers [1st ed. 1619]. Cf. S.A. Green, 2 *Proc. MHS* 11 (1897), 248. All but the *Isle of pines* were licensed. The basis for the Court's concern does not appear, but perhaps they considered these titles piracies or at any rate an inappropriate use of the College Press.

The Vincent is greatly abridged, omitting all of the moralizing of the first edition (1667). Marmaduke Johnson printed another edition in the same year from the same typographical stock. This copy is signed at the end, "William Adams His Booke Cambridge: Bought of Samuel Green february 29 1667 [1668]."

BAY PSALM BOOK *The psalms, hymns and spiritual songs of the Old Testament*
Cambridge [i.e. Amsterdam?] : Printed for H. Usher of Boston, [ca. 1680]
Usually dated 1665, following Isaiah Thomas's note in this copy. Four of the surviving seven copies, however, are bound with a 18mo Bible with an engraved t.p. dated 1648, and almost certainly printed in the Netherlands, ca. 1680. Cf. B.J. McMullin, "Format and Localization: the Eighteenmo in the Seventeenth Century," *BSANZ Bull.* 9 (1985), 139.

Lent by the American Antiquarian Society.

JOHN FOSTER, Massachusetts seal (Boston press version)

JOHN FOSTER, "Richard Mather" (two states)

AN ANNUAL CENSUS OF THE BAY PSALM BOOK (1640)

Entered by the date of the earliest recognizable published description of the copy. Changes in possession or status and the date of the change appear in curves following the first owner; subsequent public changes in ownership are recorded by an arrow (→); publicly recorded changes in private status by a hyphen; changes in classification by an equals sign.

The Old South Church Library was open to the public throughout the eighteenth century, though apparently uncatalogued and often in disorder. "Mr. [Eliezer?] Lord" made the first catalogue in 1811, though it has not survived (O.S.C. Society Book). The disorderly numbers of the 1847 catalogue, by G.H. Whitmore, already appear in a copy deposited with the Massachusetts Historical Society in 1814, and may be inherited from Lord. Shelf marks of the form "10.4.8" seem to be later; they were assigned before 13 Apr. 1849.

1810 BENTLEY → AMERICAN ANTIQUARIAN SOCIETY (1819)

Provenance: inscribed by Isaiah Thomas, "After advertising for another copy of this book, and making enquiry in many places in New-england, &c. I was not able to obtain or even hear another . . . I.T. Sept. 25th 1820."

"1640. The Psalms in Metre, Faithfully translated for the Use, Edification, and Comfort of the Saints in publick and private, especially in New England. Crown 8vo. 300 pages. An entire copy, except the title page, is now in the possession of the rev mr. [William] Bentley, of Salem . . . The book is bound in parchment"—Thomas, I, 231–2; bequeathed to Thomas or the AAS, 1819; 1837 Catalogue, fasc. P (1836), p. 43 (giving the format as 16mo); Ludewig, copy 3.

Note: t.-p. wanting; the source of Thomas's title is unknown.

1830 HARVARD COLLEGE LIBRARY

Provenance: signed (N1v) "John Leverett," perhaps the Governor, whose daughter Elizabeth married Elisha Cooke, the donor's grandfather; the gift of Middlecott Cooke (A.B. 1723), Harvard University Archives, UA III 50.27.64.2PF (VT).

"Psalms (Old) in Metre 8ᵛᵒ"—Eliot's 1765 MS. Catalogue (P); "Psalmes of David in metre. 4to <Lond. 1662 [sic] >"—1790 Catalogue, p. 188; "Psalms, Hymns, and Spiritual Songs of the Old and New Testament, faithfully translated into English Metre. 12mo. Cant. NE. 1640"—1830 Catalogue, II, 679.

Note: t.-p. wanting; the 1790 cataloguer seems to have used the imprint of the earliest known edition (London, 1652), in the White Kennett Library catalogue; the 1830 cataloguer used the title of the 2nd and later eds.

1830 OLD SOUTH CHURCH LIBRARY (MHS, 1814–59; BPL, 1866) 132 = 10.4.8 = *Prince Lib.* 21.14

Provenance: Signed and dated, t.-p. verso, "T Prince Milton Apr 9 & 10 1728"; with "*The* NEW-ENGLAND-*Library*" bookplate, inserted by Joseph Sewall after Prince's death in 1758. Prince has entered a collation of the 1647 edition in the margins.

"The whole Book of Psalms in metre. *Camb. NE* 1640—yᵉ 1st impression of the NE version"—Prince's MS. catalogue, ca. 1735; "I have found in the Old South library, and there now lies before me, the very copy of the New England version which he [Thomas Prince] made use of in preparing his Improvement, with the various changes he made written with a pen"—Wisner, p. 100; "N. England Version of Psalms"—Holmes's shelf list, shelf 7; Ludewig, copy 1; "The Whole Book of Psalmes, translated into English metre, 1640"—1847 Catalogue, pt. 2: 8vo, 132.

Note: with O.S.C. shelf marks "O.S. 132" and "10.4.8."

1847 OLD SOUTH CHURCH LIBRARY 112 → LENOX (1855) → NEW YORK PUBLIC LIBRARY (1895)

"The Whole Book of Psalms, translated into English metre, 1640 (imperfect)" —
1847 Catalogue, pt. 1: 4to, no. 112; Sotheby (William Pickering, pt. 4) 11 Jan. 1855, in lot
531 (?), or 432 (?), sold to "Holmes" (Henry Stevens); washed, perfected with twelve
leaves (W1–Y4) from O.S.C. 579, and rebound in red morocco by Francis Bedford, and
sold to James Lenox, 17 May 1855 — Stevens, p. 48–9.

Note: since the 1847 cataloguer correctly transcribed the title, the imperfection was
probably in the text; Stevens wrote 28 years after the sale, and "could not remember" the
lot number: his son suggested lot 531, and Eames conjectured lot 432. Both are odd lots
of psalm books, so the detail adds much to the illusion, but nothing to Stevens' bare
assertion. Either there is a Bay Psalm Book unaccounted for, or Stevens' "good luck" was
carefully arranged in advance. The whole romantic story is rather too good to be true, and
all the evidence has been washed away. Located at the Newberry Library in the STC
(1926), probably by a confusion of symbols (N/NY).

1847 OLD SOUTH CHURCH LIBRARY 579 (imperfect copy) = 10.4.10 → LIBRARY OF CONGRESS (1966)

"The Psalms in English metre, 1640" — 1847 Catalogue, pt. 1: 8vo, 579; released to
George Livermore by 13 Apr. 1849, when he reported its acquisition to Henry Stevens; 12
leaves were removed in 1855 and sent to Stevens to perfect the LENOX copy — Stevens, p.
48–9; consigned on the death of Livermore's widow Elizabeth with the rest of his library
(including early Bibles that had been on deposit at Harvard since 1859) to Charles F.
Libbie, 20 Nov. 1894, lot 531; sold to Alfred T. White of New York, descending to his
daughter Mrs. Adrian Van Sinderen, who deposited it in the Library of Congress in 1966
— *Quarterly Journal of the Library of Congress.*

Note: t.-p. wanting, supplied by the 1847 cataloguer from running titles; "Livermore
Books delivered to Mr. Libbie, Nov. 1894," Harvard University Archives, UA III 50.59.2,
shows that his Bay Psalm Book was never on deposit there, as is sometimes asserted;
Holmes (1940) locates the copy at the Huntington, in error. O.S.C. shelf mark "10.4.10"
on *2r; there is no evidence that the copy ever belonged to Thomas Prince.

1847 OLD SOUTH CHURCH LIBRARY 259 → YALE UNIVERSITY LIBRARY (1941)

"The Whole Book of Psalms, translated into English metre, 1640" — 1847
Catalogue, pt. 1: 8vo, 259; released to Edward Crowninshield, 1850; Leonard & Co.
(E.A. Crowninshield) 1 Nov. 1859, lot 878 (described as in "original old vellum") sold
with the rest of the library to Henry Stevens, who sold it to George Brinley, 1866, after it
had been declined by the British Museum; G.A. Leavitt (George Brinley, pt. 1) 10 Mar.
1879, lot 847, sold to Cornelius Vanderbilt, descending to his daughter (d. 1941); Parke-
Bernet (Gertrude Vanderbilt Whitney Trust) 28 Jan. 1941, bought by Rosenbach for Yale
— Farnham, p. 31; Adams (1939), p. 43; *Rosenbach*, p. 547f.

Note: Evans locates this copy in the British Library, in error. The copy has been
washed and rebound, and there are no traces of O.S.C. cataloguing.

1847 OLD SOUTH CHURCH LIBRARY 579 (perfect copy) = 10.4.10 → JOHN CARTER BROWN LIBRARY (1881)

Provenance: Richard Mather (signatures); possibly purchased by Prince at the sale of
Ephraim Baker (Samuel Mather) 30 Nov. 1737 — "Diary", p. 362–3; with "*The* New-
England-*Library*" bookplate.

"The Psalms in English Metre, 1640" — 1847 Catalogue, pt. 1: 8vo, 579; released to
N.B. Shurtleff, 1860, in exchange for some reference works (according to Shurtleff), or in
expectation of its eventual return (according to the librarian, G.F. Bigelow); Leonard &
Co. (N.B. Shurtleff Estate) 30 Nov. 1875, lot 1356, withdrawn following an injunction in a

suit for its recovery by O.S.C.; reoffered separately 12 Oct. 1876, following the court's decision against the Church, and sold to Caleb Fiske Harris of Providence (not "Senator Anthony," as stated by Littlefield); sold with other Americana to John Carter Brown on Harris' death in 1881.

Note: I have used a copy of the Leonard sale catalogue, extra-illustrated by John A. Lewis (one of Eames's authorities) with clippings from the *Boston Evening Transcript*, 19 Feb. and 9 Mar. 1876 (*penes* Michael Winship). O.S.C. shelf mark "10.4.9" on front fly-leaf.

1852 BODLEIAN LIBRARY

"1640 Psalms, in metre anonymous; no place, no name, 4to"—Cotton (1821), appending an extract; "[Psalms] faithfully translated into English metre. 4^0. *n.p.* 1640"— 1843 Catalogue (PSALMI et PSALTERIUM); "The whole Booke of Psalmes . . . 1640 . . . <Cambridge in New England, by Stephen Daye >"—Cotton, 2nd ed. (1852).

Note: Was Henry Stevens perhaps the source of Cotton's emended description? It is independent both of Thomas and of Ludewig. Bishop Tanner gave the copy in 1735.

1868 OLD SOUTH CHURCH LIBRARY (BPL, 1866) 10.4.11. = *Prince Lib.* 21.15

Provenance: "This book was bound at the cost of Mr. Ed Crowninshield and given in Exchange for no. 259 in the [1847] Catalogue. S[amuel]. T. A[rmstrong]. Jan. 1850"— pencil note on front fly-leaf; with O.S.C. shelf mark "10.4.11." Stephen Northup of North Kingstown, R.I. (d. 1687) was the volume's earliest recorded owner; it has no marks of Prince's ownership. The reason for the exchange is clearly that O.S.C. 259 was then in "collector's condition." The O.S.C. shelf mark does not necessarily disprove Armstrong's statement, as Haraszti claims; it may have been added after 1850. This copy has usually been identified with O.S.C. 112, which, however, is imperfect.

1897 HURST-CHURCH (1903)-HUNTINGTON (1911; Huntington Library and Art Gallery, 1920)

Carpenter, p. 583; Paltsits, p. 71; Dodd, Mead Catalogue 67 (April 1903); Church Catalogue 445, sold with the rest of the collection to H.E. Huntington, 1911.

1903 BRITISH LIBRARY: *see* O.S.C. 259, 1847

1926 NEWBERRY LIBRARY: *see* O.S.C. 112, 1847

1937 ROSENBACH (Rosenbach Foundation, 1953)

Bought from a Mr. Weatherup of Belfast, Northern Ireland, in 1934—Adams (1937); *Rosenbach*, p. 383–7.

1940 HUNTINGTON LIBRARY (copy 2): *see* O.S.C. 579 (imperfect copy), 1847

REFERENCES:

ADAMS, RANDOLPH G. "The Bay Psalm Book," *Colophon*, n.s. 2 (1937), 283–4.
———— *Three Americanists* (Philadelphia : Univ. of Penna. Press, 1939).
CARPENTER, EDMUND J. "The Bay Psalm Book," *New England Magazine*, n.s., 15 (1896/97), [575]–584.
Catalogus bibliothecae Harvardianae (Bostoniae : T. & J. Fleet, 1790).
Catalogue of the Library of Harvard University (Cambridge, Mass. : Metcalf, 1830).
A Catalogue of Books in the Library of the American Antiquarian Society (Worcester : H.J. Howland, 1837 [i.e. 1836–37]).
Catalogus librorum impressorum bibliothecae Bodleianae (Oxonii : E Typographo academico, 1843).
Catalogue of the Library of Rev. Thomas Prince (Boston : Crocker & Brewster, 1846 [i.e. 1847]).
CHURCH, ELIHU D. *A Catalogue of Books relating to . . . North and South America* (New York: Dodd, Mead, 1907).

COTTON, HENRY *A List of Editions of the Bible . . . in English, from the year MDV. to MDCCCXX* (Oxford : Univ. Press, 1821); 2nd ed., 1852.

ELIOT, ANDREW 1765 MS. Catalogue, Harvard University Archives UA III 50.15.31 (VT).

FARNHAM, LUTHER *A Glance at Private Libraries* (Boston : Crocker & Brewster, 1855).

HARASZTI, ZOLTÁN *The Enigma of the Bay Psalm Book* (Chicago, 1956).

HOLMES, ABIEL "Account of the Books and Manuscripts lately deposited by the Old South Church and Society . . . [1814]," MHS, Prince MSS. 20.3(3).

LIBRARY OF CONGRESS *Quarterly Journal*, 24 (1967), 204–5.

LITTLEFIELD, GEORGE E. *Early Boston Booksellers, 1642–1711* (Boston : Club of Odd Volumes, 1900).

LUDEWIG, H. "Curiosities of American Literature II," *Serapeum*, 7 (1846), 249–51.

PALTSITS, V. H. "An Account of the 'Bay Psalm Book' during the Seventeenth Century," *Literary Collector*, III, no. 3 (Dec. 1901), 69–72.

PRINCE, THOMAS "Diary," ed. A. Matthews, *PCSM* 19 (1916/17) 362–3.

———. "New-English Books & Tracts Collected by Thomas Prince of Boston NE. [ca. 1735]," MHS, Prince MSS. 20.3(1).

The Prince Library : The American Part of the Collection [Boston : Boston Pub. Lib., 1868].

Rosenbach / EDWIN WOLF, 2ND with JOHN F. FLEMING (Cleveland : World Publ., 1960).

STEVENS, HENRY *Recollections of James Lenox*, ed. V.H. Paltsits (New York : N.Y. Pub. Lib., 1951).

THOMAS, ISAIAH *The History of Printing in America* (Worcester : I. Thomas, Jr., 1810).

WALLACE, ROBERT "A Very Proper Swindle," *Life* (22 Nov. 1954), 95–106.

WISNER, BENJAMIN B. *The History of the Old South Church in Boston* (Boston : Crocker & Brewster, 1830).

JOHN FOSTER, Massachusetts seal (Cambridge press version)

THEODORE DE BRY, "Oppidum Secota"

II. PRINTING INDIAN

7. *Capital*

"The Society or Company for the Propagation of the Gospel in New England and the Parts Adjacent in America"—to give the New England Company its full name—raised and invested some £15,000, much of it expended on printing. But the New England Company interpreted its mandate broadly, spending its first £1,000 on hardware, for example, and the money served many purposes along the way. Hezekiah Usher might pay off Marmaduke Johnson's living expenses in the medium of Indian corn ("country pay") and receive a credit in London in pounds from the Company. Colonists like John Eliot and Thomas Shepard could convert cheap English-printed propaganda into expensive Indian-printed Bibles. And the presses and type that the Company paid for had a way of mingling with Harvard property after their immediate purpose was served.

NEW ENGLAND COMPANY   *Record book*, 1656–1686.
> The Company votes to send Marmaduke Johnson to Samuel Green's assistance: a mixed blessing, for he tried to seduce Green's daughter, and later set up a rival press.

ENGLAND AND WALES   *An act for the promoting and propagating the Gospel of Jesus Christ in New England*   London : E. Husband, 1649.
> The official printing, in black letter.

ENGLAND AND WALES   *An act for the promoting and propagating the Gospel of Jesus Christ in New England*   London : E. Husband, 1649.
> The private printing, in roman.

MASSACHUSETTS (Colony) GENERAL COURT   *[Order, 3 May 1676] for defraying the charges already expended upon the warre*   [Boston : J. Foster, 1676]
> The Colony seal, in the male, Boston press version; the motto, "Come over and help us," derives from the propaganda of Richard Hakluyt. It has a strange resonance in this order following King Philip's War, when the Indians of New England were finally subjugated.

THEODORE DE BRY   *Admiranda narratio, fida tamen, de commodis et incolarum ritibus Virginiae*   Francoforti ad Moenum : J. Wechel for T. de Bry, 1590.
> The Town of Secota, engraved by De Bry after John White. The Indians moved their "towns" continually, resettling in the winter, in sheltered woodland valleys, or in the fall, hunting for game. When the land was temporarily exhausted by their corn, squash and beans, they moved on, burning off new gardens. The colonists interpreted this nomadic existence as a barbarous indifference to private property and declared the land "vacant"; the Indians, who were clear enough about the boundaries of their territory, rather thought in terms of tribal sovereignty (which the colonists would not recognize).

JOHN WILSON, NATHANIEL WARD & THOMAS SHEPARD   *The day-breaking, if not the sun-rising of the Gospell with the Indians in New-England*   London : R. Cotes for F. Clifton, 1647.
> The second of eleven fund-raising tracts known as the "Eliot tracts," describing the founding of the first Indian village, Noonanetum ("Rejoicing"; now part of Newton). The General Court moved the village to Natick in 1651. Though the missions of Thomas Mayhew on Martha's Vineyard and of Richard Bourne in Plymouth Colony anticipated Eliot's, and in some ways achieved more lasting results, Eliot's genius for publicity has canonized him as *the* Apostle to the Indians.
>
> The "civilization" of the Indians began on their own initiative, when they "submitted" to the Colony in 1644. They thus gained protection against other Indians,

especially the Micmacs, secured a legal basis for their continuing existence; and received a small part of the lands they had formerly ruled *back* from the English. Best of all, the New England Company paid the colonists hard cash for "granting" these reservations. From a Congregational point of view, the tribes became the raw material for congregations, known as "praying towns", whose way of life was revolutionized. They took to shingle- and basket-making, raising cattle and hogs, building stone walls (for which they were celebrated) and making maple syrup. We can only speculate how strictly the law against biting lice was enforced, but the minister, who also served as the Colony agent, lived in Roxbury, fifteen long miles away. Like most congregations, the Indians (within obvious limits) remained a law to themselves. It has been suggested that their Mosaic tripartite organization (based on Exodus 18:25), covertly encouraged traditional Indian political forms to survive.

JOHN WILLIAMS   *The redeemed captive, returning to Zion*   Boston : B. Green for S. Phillips, 1707.
Williams and his family were captured by a Mohawk raiding party and taken to Quebec, where his daughter Eunice converted to Roman Catholicism and married an Indian. To everyone's credit, the two sides of the family kept in touch after her conversion and marriage.

8. Real Characters

The role of print in converting the Indians was not necessarily limited to the alphabet, though the logocentric New Englanders saw no other way. The Jesuits engraved the Bible story in pictures for the use of missionaries. The Indians themselves used pictographs, which the Recollect fathers in Nova Scotia successfully elaborated as a mnemonic for religious texts. Syllabaries afforded a simpler scheme for representing Algonquian languages than the alphabet. None of these alternatives was as invasive of Indian culture as the alphabet, which inevitably represented the White Man's version of Indian languages, not what the Indians thought, heard and spoke. "Ciiśaś" (pronounced "Cheesus"), and King "Chouch", Third of that name, are authentically Indian figures.

COTTON MATHER   *The wonderful works of God commemorated*   Boston : S. Green, 1690.
The woodcut is Mather's impression of the pictographs on Dighton Rock, on the Taunton River; even Cotton Mather, for once in his life, was stumped. Later writers have discovered Phoenician, Chinese, and Old Norse messages, and "MIGVEL CORTEREAL V DEI HIC DUX IND". See for yourself.

JOHN WILKINS   *An essay towards a real character and a philosophical language*
London : S. Gellibrand and J. Martyn, 1668.
Wilkins drew "real characters" to represent ideas, assigning them phonetic values for proper names; the 160 sorts were cut by Joseph Moxon for this book.

Christmas hymns (Micmac hieroglyphic MS), ca. 1750.
These characters were devised by Fathers Chrétien Le Clercq and Pierre Maillard, building on native pictographs. The system remained in use down to the nineteenth century, despite the best efforts of Protestant missionaries.

The good book, containing the hymnal = Buch das gut, enthaltend den Gesang   Wien : K.K. Buchdruckerei, 1866.
Kyrie eleison, in Micmac hieroglyphic: note IHS for Jesus and the trinitarian Triangle for

COTTON MATHER *The wonderful works of God commemorated*

God. This is the first and last printed edition, by the Redemptorist Christian Kauder. There are 5703 sorts, some of them (such as the symbols for the K.K. Buchdruckerei) devised for this edition, most of which perished in a shipwreck coming over. The type was never used again.

GERÓNIMO NADAL *Adnotationes et meditationes in Evangelia qvae in sacrosancto Missae sacrificio toto anno legvntvr* Antuerpiae : M. Nutius, 1595 [i.e. 1596]
The plates were also separately issued in 1596, with title: *Evangelicae historiae imagines.* These engravings by the Wierix brothers were used by missions as far apart as Quebec and China. The Colbert-Hoym copy.

SEQUOYAH (George Guess) *Cherokee alphabet* [Boston : American Board of Commissioners for Foreign Missions, ca. 1838]; & S.A. WORCESTER, "RWhET [read 'Svlanigvi']," MS world map lettered in Cherokee syllabary, 1838.
Sequoyah used the alphabet, but assigned it different phonetic values, and added supplemental characters. His syllabary was so successful that even the missionaries adopted it. The system is still in use for native religion and medicine, but even in Sequoyah's time the official language of the tribe was English.
Deposited by the United Church Board for World Ministries.

Der Weġ _ die Wahrheit _ das Leben. _

NEW TESTAMENT (Cree) *Ośki Tistemint tipeyicikeminaw miina ki pimaaciyieyminaw Ciiśaś Karyśt* ["The New Testament of our Lord and Savior Jesus Christ"] London : British and Foreign Bible Society, 1862.
This is the second Bible in an American Indian language, translated under the supervision of William Mason and first printed in London, 1859.

The syllabary was devised by the Wesleyan Methodist James Evans, and is still in use (it appears on publications of Air Canada). Vowels are indicated by rotation of the symbol, which allowed Evans to use a single punch for four different syllables. In the current system, there are only 9 sorts and 15 "appendages" (diacritics) for indicating consonants at the end of a syllable. Casting type in lead from the lining of tea chests, in matrices carved from oak, dabbing them with ink made of sturgeon oil and soot, and printing on a fur press, Evans managed to produce some 2000 pages, 1840–41.

DOMINICA SEXAGESIMAE
Parabola Seminantis.
Matt. xiij. Marc. iiij. Luc. viij.   Anno xxxij.

38

xvij

B.Paſſ. Rom. inv.   *Ant.Wierx ſculp*

A. IESVS ſedens in naui, ad lit=
    tus iuxta Capharnaum, docet.
B. Agricola ſementem faciens.
C. Cadit ſemen in viam.
D. Cadit in petroſa.

E. Cadit in ſpinetum.
F. Cadit in terram bonam, & facit
    vnum, centeſimum fructum,
    aliud, ſexageſimum, &c.
    Parabolam explicat Chriſtus.

Antonie Wierix, "Parabola seminantis"

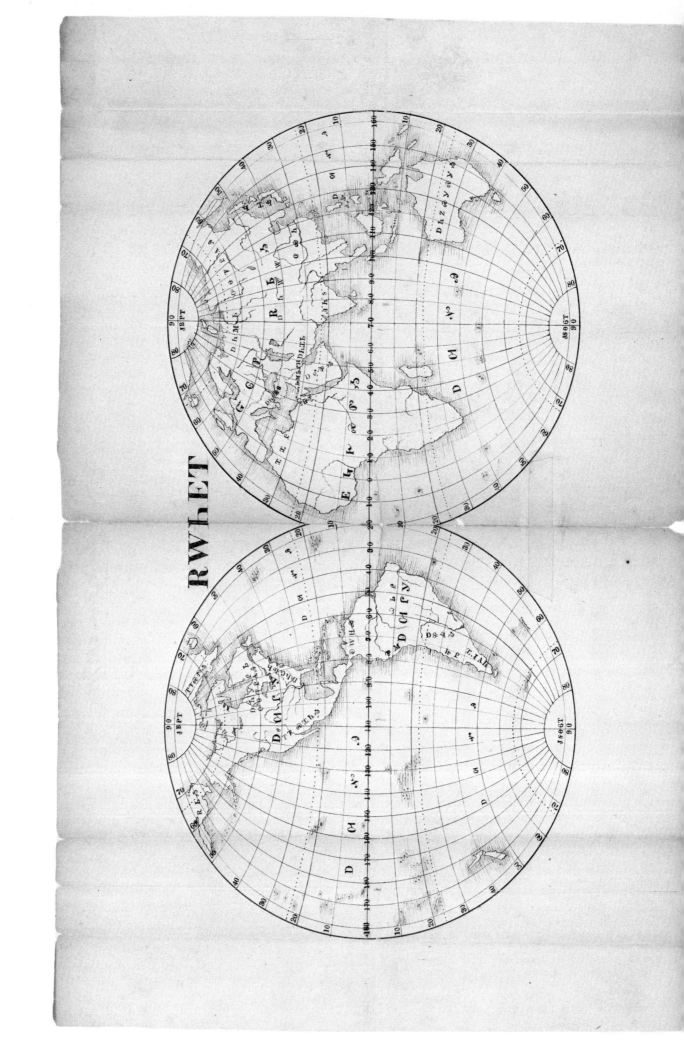

ᐅᐢᑭ

ᑎᐢᑌᒥᐣᐟ

ᑭ ᑎᐯᔨᐦᒋᑫᒥᓇᐤ ᒦᓇ ᑭ ᐱᒫᒋᔨᐍᒥᓇᐤ

ᒌᓴᐢ ᑲᕒᐧᐢᐟ.

ᐁ ᒦᐢᑯᒋᐃᑕᓯᓇᐊᐠ ᓀᐃᔭᐍᐃᐧᓂˣ

ᐃᓯ

ᐃᐧᕑᕑᔭᒼ ᒣᓱᐣ, ᐊᔭᒥᐁᐃᐧᑭᒫᐤ.

LONDON:
PRINTED BY W. M. WATTS
FOR THE
BRITISH AND FOREIGN BIBLE SOCIETY,
10, EARL STREET, BLACKFRIARS.

1862.

New Testament (Cree)

9. Alphabets and Language

The alphabet is phonetically redundant even for English, and more so for Algonquian languages, which do not distinguish voiced and voiceless stops (i.e. *bdg* from *ptk*). Letter frequencies are also different, so that printers needed more k's, and depending on dialect, no l, or r, or n. Unlike Father Rale, who tried to spell what the Indians pronounced, the New England translators spelled borrowed English words English fashion (e.g. wheat, barley, silver, gold). Eliot's solution for translating the Bible is ultimately a device for teaching the Indians English; but the colonists begrudged even this expedient. Not a penny was ever raised in New England for the conversion of the Indians.

JOHANN RIEMER *Über-reicher Schatz-meister aller hohen Standes und bürgerliche Freud- und Leid-complimente* Leipzig und Franckfurt : C. Lunitzius, 1690.
The motto under the frontispiece may be translated "Speak, that I may see thee"; the writer demonstrates his eloquence on the facing title-page.

Sébastien Rale, "Les animaux"

Sébastien Rale *Abenaki-French dictionary*, compiled 1691 – 1723.

This volume was looted in a raid on Father Rale's mission in Norridgewock, Maine, in 1723; the colonist went back the next year, murdered the author, and brought his scalp back to Boston. Rale used a greek ou ligature for Eliot's oo (both transcribed here as 8). The volume is open to a list of animals, showing some familiar borrowings in Indian from English, such as ká8s [cows], pl. ká8s8k and ahas8k$_8$ (from "horse"); and in English from Indian, such as m8s [moose] and ségañk$_8$ [skunk]. Evidently the Abenaki had also seen a monkey.

INNOKENTIĬ, Metropolitan of Moscow   *Nachatki khristīanskago uchenīia* = *Khristianam" achigloigan" itaṅgisiṅgin"* ["Primer of Christian doctrine"]   Sanktpeterburg : Sẏnodal'naĩa Tipografīĩa, 1840.
Facing Russian (in civil type) and Aleut (in church type) with a special ng ligature; translated by Ivan Venĩaminov and Jakob Netsvietov. Peter the Great introduced civil type in Russia in 1707.

ROGER WILLIAMS   *A key into the language of America*   London : G. Dexter, 1643.
Presenting a paraphrase of Genesis.

WILLIAM WOOD   *Nevv Englands prospect*   London : T. Cotes for J. Bellamy, 1635.
"There is no L"; the conventions of English spelling, however, were regularly applied to Massachusett — such as final -ck for k, ch for č and sh for š, doubling of consonants to indicate short vowels, etc. And loan words required an L, and an R too, unless one were to write, say, "Febnuany," as the Indians did. So there was an L anyhow.

JOHN ELIOT   *The Indian grammar begun*   Cambridge : M. Johnson, 1666.
Written as an introduction for the officers of the New England Company; using English stems to represent Indian paradigms (e.g. "me get-um").
The alphabet: the oo ligature was more familiar in black-letter printing.

The A.B.C. with the catechisme   London: Company of Stationers, 1605.
ABC's were in black letter down to 1640. After 1679, the schooling of Indian children was in English.

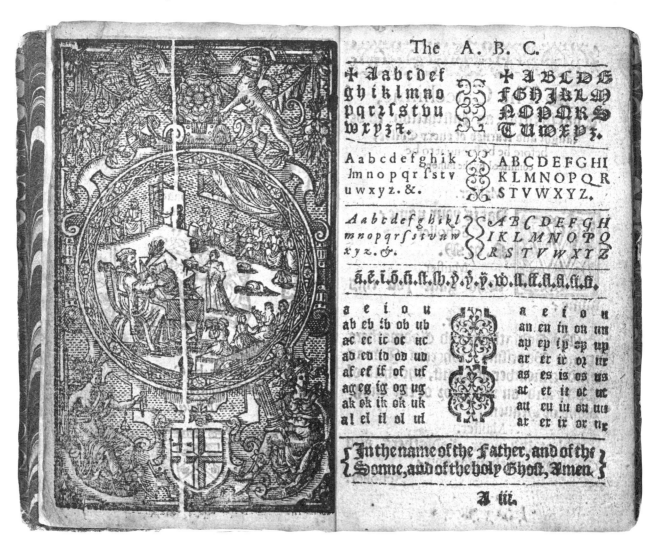

LEWIS BAYLY *Manitompae pomantamoonk* ["Godly living"] Cambridge : [M. Johnson], 1665.
>Signed "nen Simon" and on later pages "nen Simon Papenau" (literally "I Simon Papenau") by the Mashpee Indian Simon Papenau or Papenah (fl. 1750), with his annotations throughout. His Indian Bible survives in the American Philosophical Society (transcribed and translated by I. Goddard and K. J. Bragdon, *Native Writings in Massachusett* [Philadelphia : American Philosophical Soc., 1988], I, 420). Algonquian languages "conjugated" nouns, so that a native speaker could not idiomatically sign plain "Simon Papenau"; thus the Jesuits, after some thought, devised the Indian baptismal formula, "In the name of Our Father, of His Son, and of Their Holy Ghost." Note that Papenau's alphabet owes nothing to Eliot, omitting "Ch."

JOHANNES AMOS COMENIUS *Ianua aurea reserata (Greek & Latin)* Amstelodami : L. Elzevir, 1649.
>Annotated "Joell Iacoomis his Booke 4s." by the eldest son of Hiacoomes, the first Indian convert on Martha's Vineyard. "A hopeful young prophet" (Gookin, *Hist. Colls.*, p. 15), Joel would have graduated from Harvard in 1665, but was murdered by the Nantucket Indians on a trip home.
>
>Harvard's efforts (if that is not too strong a word) to educate an Indian ministry have evoked amusement, at the spectacle of redskins receiving a classical education, and scorn, for the smug belief (not wholly extinct today) that a Harvard education is its own reward. Perhaps no education could survive these criticisms, which appeal to Hannah More's affection for the *status quo*, on the one hand, and Mr. Gradgrind's hopes for an efficient workforce, on the other. Ironically, Comenius himself held no brief for language and literature as such. And perhaps the "New England Way" of Congregationalism is as much at fault as Greek and Latin. So few openings did the Colony afford a minister, that a third of Harvard's first 100 graduates (excluding the weak-minded William Mildmay) re-migrated to England, and others, like Increase Mather, vacillated. The Indians were even more impoverished than the cowboys, even with subventions from the New England Company, and by the end of the eighteenth century turned to the more affordable persuasion of Baptism.

10. The Indian Press

The Eliot Indian Bible is the largest single project of any press in North America before Samuel Willard's *Compleat Body of Divinity*, published by subscription in 1726. The 938 reams of paper (over 300,000 sheets) consumed in two editions of the Bible probably outweigh all the previous printing in English together. For Bibles alone, the New England Company was out of pocket about £1,825 in all—around £70 a year, which compares pretty favorably with the average annual budget of Harvard at this date, of about £265. There were only 1100 praying Massachusetts in 1674, and they suffered great losses in King Philip's War; even including the Indians in Plymouth Colony and Nope (Martha's Vineyard), the Company printed about one Bible for every 2.5 Christian Indians (man, woman and child) in Massachusetts.

This may seem unrealistic to a generation that has read the Bible once, if at all. And in general, most historians dismiss the Eliot Indian Bible as unintelligible, even to the Indians, or simply as a blatant tool for cultural destruction. This may be just another way of saying that the Indians could not, or did not "really" want to read it; but the facts refute such condescension. Another edition was called for in only twenty-four years; the dialect of the Indians on Nope gradually conformed to Massachusett; and the Mashpee Indians were still clinging to their copies in the nineteenth century. The copies that survive are nearly all white men's—who *certainly* found them difficult to read—and they have generalized from this experience. A new census of copies is badly needed, on which we can build a better understanding of the place of the Bible in Indian society, and the New England economy. If nothing else, the Indian Bible was a seventeenth-century equivalent of a neighborhood General Motors plant.

JOHANN HEINRICH GOTTFRIED ERNESTI *Die wol-eingerichtete Buchdruckereÿ*
Nürnberg : A. Endters Sohn und Erben, 1721.
The two-press printing house probably reflects what the Indian College looked like, when
the Eliot Indian Bible was printing.

NEW TESTAMENT (Massachusett) *Wusku wuTestamentum nul-Lordumun Jesus
Christ = The New Testament of our Lord and Savior Jesus Christ* Cambridge :
S. Green [, M. Johnson, & J. Printer], 1661.
Translated under the supervision of John Eliot by Job Nesutan. Algonquian languages
distinguish two classes of noun: animate, which includes some plants like tobacco, that
have "power"; and inanimate, containing most plants and inorganic substances. The
borrowed word "Testament" (the -um ending indicates a possessed noun: his Testament)
is animate; a useful distinction, for a religious people.

BIBLE (Massachusett) *Mamusse wunneetupanatamwe up-Biblum God* ["All of
God's Holy Bible"] Cambridge : S. Green[, M. Johnson & J. Printer], 1663.
Open to Genesis, 24:3, "And I will make thee swear by the LORD the God of heaven, and
the God of the earth, that thou shalt not take a wife unto my sonne of the daughters of
the Canaanites among whom I dwell." Nesutan uses Keitannit ("The Great Spirit',
"Manitou") to translate "the God of heaven" and "the God of the earth."

CONSTANTINE SAMUEL RAFINESQUE *The American nations* Philadelphia : C.S.
Rafinesque, 1836.
The beginning of the Delaware *Walum Olam* ("Red Score"), containing the creation by
the Great Spirit, Kitanowit; the text was originally written pictographically on sticks, and
survives only in Rafinesque's transcription and translation.
Lent by the Arnold Arboretum.

GEORGE PARKER WINSHIP *The first American Bible* Boston : Merrymount Press, 1929.
As this leaf from the original text shows ("silver kah gold"), the translation was from
English, not from Hebrew or Greek. One might also note—though it is harder to
illustrate—that there are aural errors that Eliot would have been unlikely to commit (such
as "ball-headed" for "bald-headed").

BIBLE (Massachusett) *The Holy Bible* Cambridge : S. Green and M. Johnson [& J.
Printer], 1663.
One of twenty presentation copies sent to Roger Boyle, the head of the New England
Company; bound in contemporary black morocco, gilt, by the London stationer Samuel
Gellibrand (William Kellaway, *The New England Company, 1649–1776* [1961], p. 133, n. 3).
Two other copies survive in identical bindings.
Lent by Roxbury Latin School.

BIBLE (Massachusett) *Mamusse wunneetupanatamwe up-Biblum God*, Nahohtôeu
ontchetôe printeu8muk ["2nd ed., corr."] Cambridge : S. Green [& J. Printer],
1685.
Revised by John Eliot and John Cotton.

COTTON MATHER *India Christiana* Boston : B. Green, 1721.
A proposal to print a third edition of the Massachusett Bible elicited new types and paper
from the New England Company; which the Bostonians appropriated to other purposes.
As Mather points out, you can just as well and much more cheaply be Christian in
English. He here proposes to extend these methods to Malabar.

A NOTE ON THE PRINTER
AND TRANSLATOR

JAMES PRINTER (Wowaus), d. 1717.

Nipmuck, son of Naoas, deacon (sachem?) at Hassanamesit (f. 1671); apprenticed to Samuel Green, 1659, for what was to prove a record term. Teacher at Waeuntug (now part of Uxbridge) 1669–74, when Gookin reports that he could "read well, and, as I take it, write also" (*Hist. Colls.*, p. 45). Evidently, he was no longer living with his master, though he was still considered his apprentice. In 1675–76, he fought with King Philip, declaring bitterly, on surrendering, "that more Indians had dyed since this *War* began of diseases (such as at other times they used not to be acquainted withal) than by the Sword of the English" (Hubbard, p. 96). After the war, he resettled in Natick, where he appears as signatory in a deed of the "Nipmug country" to William Stoughton and Joseph Dudley, 1682 (facsimile in Trumbull, p. 477). The act implies a measure of political authority, and perhaps Printer had succeeded his father, who was already 80 years old in 1674, as sachem. Gookin describes him as a "press man" in 1674, but his skills were broader, for in 1683 Eliot wrote to Robert Boyle, "We have but one man (*viz.* the Indian printer [sic]) that is able to compose the sheets, and correct the press, with understanding" (1 *Colls. MHS*, 3 [1810], 181). He later returned to Hassanamesit, where he was teacher to five families in 1698, continuing to his death in 1717. He appears in an imprint for the first and last time in the *Massachuset Psalter* (1709), having performed his articles at last, after 50 years. His widow Mary, two sons, "Ami" (i.e. Ammi) and Moses, and a grandson Ammi Jr. survived him, and grant the bulk of Hassanamesit to the township of Grafton in 1728, signing with their initials. The Printer family continued farming there down to the nineteenth century, and a remnant of their reservation, Hassanamisco, still survives.

Hubbard calls him "*James* the *Printer*, the *Superadded Title* distinguishing him from others of that name"; implying that the title was given by the English. It may equally well be Indian, marking his mastery of an exceptional skill. "All their names are significant and variable," wrote Edward Winslow in 1624, "for when they come to the state of men and women, they alter them according to their deeds or dispositions." The identification of James Printer with the little Indian James, whom the General Court parked on President Dunster in 1645, must be rejected. The Nipmucks did not "submit" to English jurisdiction until 1649, and would hardly have entrusted their children to an open enemy.

SOURCES:

DENIS A. CONNOLE, "Land Occupied by the Nipmuck Indians of Central New England, 1600–1700," *Bull. of the Mass. Archeological Soc.*, 38 (1976) 14.

SAMUEL G. DRAKE, *Biography and History of the Indians of North America*, 11th ed. (Boston: B.B. Mussey, 1851), p. 114–5 and 180.

SAMUEL ELIOT MORISON, *The Founding of Harvard College* (Cambridge, Mass.: Harvard Univ. Press, 1935), p. 313.

FREDERICK C. PIERCE, *History of Grafton* (Worcester: C. Hamilton, 1879).

Records of the Governor and Company of the Massachusetts Bay in New England, ed. N.B. Shurtleff, v. 5 (1674–86) (Boston: W. White, 1854), p. 368.

J.H. TRUMBULL, "The Indian Tongue and its Literature as Fashioned by Eliot and Others," *Memorial History of Boston*, ed. Justin Winsor (Boston: J.R. Osgood, 1885), I, 477.

FREDERICK L. WEIS, "The New England Company of 1649 and its Missionary Enterprises," *PCSM* 38 (1948), 134–218.

GEORGE PARKER WINSHIP, *The Cambridge Press, 1638–1692* (Philadelphia: Univ. of Penna Press, 1945).

JOB NESUTAN (d. 1675)

Entered Harvard before 1665, but did not take a degree, though he is described as "a towardly lad and apt witt for a scholler"; preacher at Okkokonimesit (f. 1654; later Marlborough) 1669–1675; he was "a very good linguist in the English tongue, and was

Mr. Eliot's assistant and interpreter in his translation of the Bible, and other books of the Indian language" (Gookin, p. 444). He died at Mount Hope (later Bristol, R.I.), 6 July 1675, fighting for the United Colonies against King Philip.

Not to be confused (as he regularly is) with Eliot's first interpreter, a Montauk, probably one Cockenoe. John Sassamon, Indian protomartyr-provocateur, is also said to have assisted in the translation of the Bible (Drake, p. 193), but not on any contemporary authority.

SOURCES:

Daniel Gookin, "An Historical Account of the Doings and Sufferings of the Christian Indians in New England," *Archaeologia Americana*, 2 (1836) 422–534.

S.E. Morison, *Harvard College in the Seventeenth Century* (Cambridge: Harvard Univ. Press, 1936), I, 356 n.2 (identifying the Harvard "lad" as John Wampus, a married man of no scholarly distinction).

W.W. Tooker, *John Eliot's First Indian Teacher and Interpreter* (New York: Harper, 1896).

Frederick L. Weis, "The New England Company of 1649," p. 172.

Cambridge University seal

III. LEGAL ISSUES

1. *Vacuum domicilium cedit occupanti*

CORPUS JURIS CIVILIS, ed. Jacques Cujas   Aureliae : E. Gamonet for T. de Juges, 1625. 6v.

The text in the center of the page is surrounded with the gloss of Accursius; whose gloss is annotated in its turn by the commentary of Godefroy and Conti in the margins; a digest of interpretations *variorum* by Pierre Brossé is appended at the end of each volume except the sixth, which contains an index to the whole by Esteban Daoyz. Various volumes of this edition appear in the 1723 Harvard Library catalogue, under the headings "Corpus," "Digestum," *"Dayoz"*, *"Justinianus"*, and "Infortiatum."

JOHN COTTON   *The bloudy tenent, washed, and made white in the bloud of the Lambe*
London : M. Symmons, 1647.

Rejecting Roger Williams' contention that the Indians did not neglect their land, but improved the soil by annual burnings, and citing the maxim *"Vacuum domicilium cedit occupanti"* ("An empty dwelling-place is free for the taking") to justify the Puritan landgrab. The position was precarious, since it meant that anyone (Roger Williams, for example) might appropriate land you had your eye on; and the colonists also fell back on a rationale of conquest, and the Biblical injunction to be fruitful and multiply. Ultimately Cotton's doctrine derives from Civil Law or the Talmud, which founders of international law like Grotius and Selden extended from the private to the public domain; but the immediate source of the maxim is still unknown.

Sir EDWARD COKE   *La sept part des Reports*   [London] : Soc. of Stationers, 1608.

Open to Calvin's Case; justifying the taking of land by conquest from the heathen. In Coke's classic restatement of English law, any vacant land belonged to the King, so that the colonists could only acquire title by royal patent.

WILLIAM WOOD   *Nevv Englands prospect*   London : T. Cotes for J. Bellamy, 1634.

The invasion of America took place at all levels: by epidemics, which removed 80–90% of the native human population; by trade, which changed subsistence hunters into commercial trappers and made self-sufficient communities dependent on imports; by cattle, sheep and swine, which replaced Indian moose and deer; and by the conversion of forest into pasture and cropland, destroying the habitat of game. By 1700, even Indians who had not "submitted" were wearing cloth and raising cattle and swine. Perhaps the ultimate irony is that Eliot needn't have bothered. The map shows the score in 1634: seven English towns to three Indian.

NATHANIEL MORTON   *New-England's memoriall*   Cambridge : Printed by S. G[reen]. and M. J[ohnson]. for J. Usher, 1669.

Unlike the Puritans, the Pilgrims entered into treaties with the Indians; there were more Indians and fewer Pilgrims then, and the Pilgrims had no Royal patent.

MASSACHUSETTS (Colony)   *A copy of the Kings Majesties charter for incorporating the Company of the Massachusetts Bay . . . granted . . . 1628*   Boston : S. Green for B. Harris, 1689.

The Glorious Revolution raised hopes, reflected in this edition, that Massachusetts might recover its Charter, revoked by Charles II; but the Province charter (1691) submitted the Colony to English jurisdiction and ended its territorial adventures.

The original patent was for the land between the Merrimac and Charles Rivers, from coast to coast. The Province incorporated New Plymouth, the Manor of Tisbury and Lord-

in fructu:& ſic ſuum eſſe credit. nam poſſeſſor vſucapere poteſt has res:nec dicitur fieri furtum,cum non ſit affectus furandi. & h. d.hæc l. cum prin.ſequen.Fr.

a ¶ Alienauerit.vt Inſti. eo.§.ſed tamen. & ſ.manda.l.mandatũ. & idem in ſimilibus vbi iuſtus eſt error: vt ſ.manda.l.mandatũ.

¶ Sed numquid ipſe heres per ſe vſucapiet? Reſpo.non. quia perſonali actione tenetur. ſed nulla eſt ratio: vt ſ.eo.l pignori.§ fin. Sed ea ratio eſt,quia videtur à non bonam fidẽ habere,cum in eius locum ſucceſſit qui bonam fidem non habebat,non h̄dico malam: vt ſ̄ de diuer.praeſcri.l. cum heres. & tacit ſ.de adqui.here.l. cum quidam.§.quod ſi ipſe.

¶ Item nonne poſſeſſionem deponens,& ſi alij tradita ſit,retinet? Reſpon.non. vt ſ.cod. l.non ſolum.§.qui pignori.& ſ.tit.1.l.38.quod & ſeruus. maxime rei mobilis.Acc.

b ¶ Crediderit. vt ſi authoris cenſetur quis ſit inſtitutus heres,& poſtea ſit mutatum teſtamentum.Acc.

c ¶ Exiſtimans.ſcilicet errore iuris. & ſic eſt contra ſ.l.nunqua. in prin. Sol.ſ.loquitur de eo qui per errorem iuris credit:at ſi ẽ in errore,iuris iuſti eſſe,cum ipſo iure nullus ſit:hic loquitur de illo qui errat in facto,quia credebat fructuariũ proprietarium eſſe. 2.Vel hic non fuit error ex iuris inducens ignorantis. 3.Vel malam fidem in vſucapionibus & praeſcriptionibus, non intelligitur nec refertur ad malam fidem fictã heredis.v.plura apud Balbum tract.de praeſcri. 3 part.1 q.3.

alienauerit a. 1. ¶ Item ſi quis aliqua exiſtimatione deceptus crediderit b ad ſe hereditatem pertinere.quæ ad eum non pertineat,& rem hereditariam alienauerit : aut ſi is ad quem vſusfructus ancillæ pertinet , partum e ius exiſtimans ſuum eſſe, quia & ſætus pecudum ad fructuariũ pertinet , alienauerit.

Si res cuius poſſeſſio ciuilis & naturalis vacat . clandeſtine occupetur , non efficietur per hoc vitioſa vitio reali,ſed perſonali: & ideo licet occupans non poſſit vſucapere, vel praeſcribere propter ſuam malam fidem,per alium tamen bona fidei poſſeſſore cum tit.poterit praeſcribi, & dicitur vacare ciuilis vel naturalis,vel per negligentiam cõmiſſa in recuperando naturalẽ: vel quia poſſeſſor deceſſit ſine herede:vel per obliuionem quæ inducitur per lapſũ longi temporis.h.d.

XXXVII. Idem libro ſecundo Inſtitutionum.

FVrtum non cõmittitur. Furtum enim ſine affectu furandi nõ committitur c.1. ¶ Fundi quoque alieni poteſt aliquis ſine vi naſciſci poſſeſſionem,quæ vel ex negligentia d domini vacet,vel quia dominus ſine ſucceſſore deceſſerit g , vel longo h tempore abfuerit i.

XXXVIII. Idem libro ſecundo Rerum cottidianarum ſiue aureorum.

QVam rem * ipſe quidem non poteſt vſucapere : quia intelligit alienum ſe poſſidere, & ob id mala fide poſſidet. Sed ſi alij bona fide accipienti tradiderit k, poterit is vſucapere l : quia neque vi poſſeſſum,neque furtiuum poſſidet. Abolita eſt enim quorumdam veterum ſententia, exiſtimantium etiam fundi loci...

ve m furtum fieri ¶.

Pone hic caſum, quod quis occupauit ſolum per vim,poſtea ibi ipſe vel alius ædificauit : deinde ad te peruenit ſolum & ſuperficies bona fide & titulo.certum eſt quod ſolũ non potes praeſcribere: quia eſt affectum vitio reali. An ſaltem ædificium? & dicitur quod non:intelligo verum reſpectu directi dominy:ſed reſpectu vtilis,ſi poſſedit tamquam ſuperficiarius, videtur ſecus. P.de Cast.

XXXIX. Marcianvs libro tertio Inſtitutionum.

SI ſolum v vſucapi non poterit : nec ſuperficies p vſucapietur.

Per hereditatem iacentem vſucapio cæpta per defunctum poteſt cõplers, & ſine poſſeſſione. Pav.

XL. Nerativs libro quinto Regularum.

COeptam q vſucapionem à defuncto poſſe & ante aditam hereditatem impleri , conſtitutum eſt r.*

Vitium furti vel violentia non purgatur , licet res veniat in poteſtatem procuratoris. P.de Cast.

XLI. Idem libro ſeptimo Membranarum.

SI rem ſubreptam mihi procurator r meus adprehendit, quamuis per procuratorem poſſeſſionem apiſci non iam ferè conueniat: nihilo magis x eam in poteſtatem meam rediſſe, vſuque y capi poſſe z exiſtimarum eſt : quia contra ſtatui a, captioſum erit b.

Si venditor ſuccedat domino rei furtiua vel dotalis , vitium reale purgatur.Bart.

XLII. Papinianvs libro tertio Quæſtionum.

CVm vir prædium dotale c vendidit ſcienti vel ignoranti...

(margin) f.Nouum.

The South part of Nevv-England, as it is Planted this yeare, 1634.

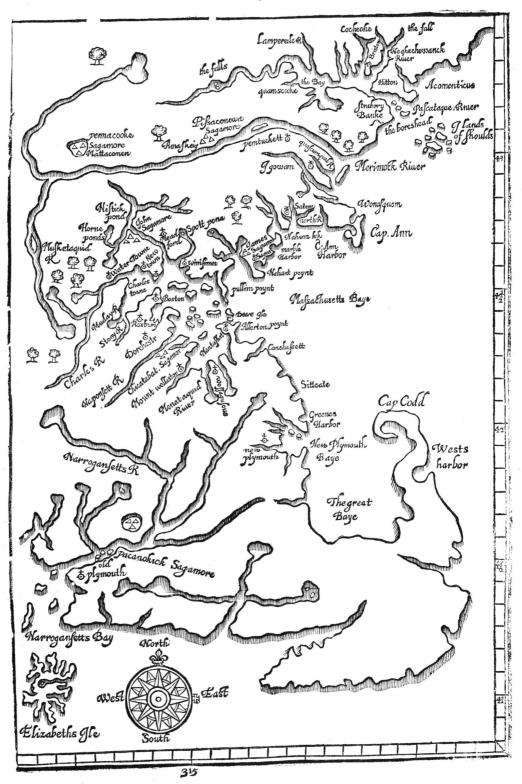

315

WILLIAM WOOD
Nevv Englands prospect

ship of Martha's Vineyard, and Maine with the original grant, whose expansion westward was ended by the conquest of New Amsterdam in 1664. At various times, with indifferent success, the patentees had grasped for parts of New Hampshire, Connecticut and Rhode Island. Indian deeds, whose validity they rejected within the borders of their patent, could provide pretexts for aggression outside of it, or indeed defenses against the authority of the Crown.

2. Harvard College Library

The Library catalogue of 1723 lists only twelve Anglo-American lawbooks, mostly statutes; there were vastly more works of Roman and Civil law. The bequest of Serjeant John Maynard's library in 1682 ought to have strengthened Harvard's legal collections, but evidently it did not include his professional books. The Law Library split off in 1818, and in *its* first catalogue (1834), Charles Sumner observed that some of the former civil and canon law books were still desiderata. He also notes many copies in the collection associated with Robert Auchmuty, Jeremiah Gridley, James Otis and Samuel Sewall (d. 1751), from the gift of Christopher Gore (1822). It would be interesting to reassemble the Gore gift, and perhaps Justice Story's library as well, which Harvard received shortly afterward. The standard study of colonial law libraries, by Herbert Johnson, unfortunately ignores these sources, which often provide concrete information on use as well as evidence of access. All the titles in this case appear in the 1723 Catalogue, though only one Ishmael survived a fire of 1764.

HARVARD COLLEGE   *Catalogus librorum bibliothecae Collegij Harvardini*   Boston : B. Green, 1723.
Open to the entry for Coke on Littleton, 1670.

Sir EDWARD COKE   *The first part of the Institutes of the laws of England,* 7th ed. London: J. Streater, [etc.] for G. Sawbridge, [etc.], 1670.
The gift of the Boston bookseller John Usher, in the 17th century; with the call no. of the 1723 catalogue, 18.2.13, on the t.-p. The volume apparently survived the fire of 1764 that destroyed the College Library because it was "on loan" (to P. Chardin? whose signature appears at the top of the t.-p., 1757).

ENGLAND AND WALES   *The Statutes at large / by Joseph Keble*   London : Assigns of J. Bill, [etc.], 1684.
The gift of Middlecott Cooke, 1764; perhaps from Elisha Cooke's library.

Sir HENRY SPELMAN   *Concilia, decreta, leges, constitutiones, in re ecclesiarum orbis Britannici*   London : F. Badger, [etc.], 1639.

ENGLAND AND WALES   *The whole volume of Statutes at large . . . since Magna Charta, vntill XXIX. Elizabeth*   London : C. Barker, 1587.
This edition (with a supplement of Sessions Acts down to 4 Chas. I) was among the books given by John Harvard in 1636. His copy, unfortunately, perished in the fire of 1764.

MICHAEL DALTON   *The country justice*   London: W. Rawlins and S. Roycroft, to be sold by S. Keble, 1690.
This is the only treatise of the office of J.P. that carried authority in the courts. The copy is inscribed by the purchaser, Benjamin Whitman, "Bought of the Honble David Hewett Esq. Att^y General of the State of Rd island Providence Sept. 5th 1789."

Liber Bibliothecus

The First Part

OF THE

INSTITUTES

Of the Laws of

ENGLAND.

OR,

A Commentary upon LITTLETON, not the name of the
Author only, but of the LAW it self.

MARTIAL.
Quid te vana juvant miseræ ludibria Chartæ?
Hoc lege, quod possit dicere jure meum est.

CICERO.
Major hæreditas venit unicuique nostrum à
Jure & Legibus, quàm à Parentibus.

Hæc ego grandævus posui tibi, candide Lector.

Authore EDWARDO COKE Milite.

The Seventh Edition carefully Corrected.

LONDON,

Printed by **John Streater, James Flesher,** and **Henry Twyford**, Assigns of
Richard Atkins and **Edward Atkins**, Esquires.

And are to be sold by *George Sawbridge, John Place, John Bellinger, William Place,*
Thomas Basset, Robert Pawlet, Christopher Wilkinson, Thomas Dring, William Jacob,
Allen Banks, Ch. Harper, John Amery, John Poole, John Leigh, MDCLXX.

Cum Gratia & Privilegio Regiæ Majestatis.

An Exact Catalogue of the Common & Statute Law Book[s] of this Realm, and some others relating thereunto

Be pleased to take Notice, That F. signifies French Law, and L. Latine, the rest are English; And where there is any difference in the Editi[on] this Mark * is prefixed.

		l.	s.	d.
	A			
F.	Andersons Reports, 2 parts Fol	0	14	0
F.	Ashes Tables to the Law Fol	1	0	0
F.	—Tables to Cooks Reports Fol	0	6	0
	—The same in English 8°	0	6	0
F	—Epieiceia 8°	0	2	0
F	—Table to Dyer Fol.	0	2	6
	—Fasciculus Florum 8°	0	1	0
	Argum. on the Writ of Hab. Corpus	0	1	0
	Argument concerning the Militia.	0	0	6
	Assize of Bread 4°	0	0	6
L.	Astons Placita Lat. Rediviv 4°	0	6	0
	Andrews Argument at his Tryal 4°	0	1	0
F.	Abr. Book of Assizes 8°	0	1	6
	Attourney of the Common Pleas	0	1	6
	Abridgment Hen. 7. 8°	0	5	6
	Attourneys Guide 8°	0	2	0
	B			
L.	Bracton Folio	0	16	0
L.	—Quarto	0	12	0
F.	Brooks Abridgment, large Folio	1	10	0
F.	—Small Folio	1	15	0
F.	—Quarto	2	5	0
	—Reading on Limitation 8°	0	1	6
	—Reading on Magna Charta 4°	0	0	6
F.	—Cases 8°	0	1	6
	—The same in English 8°	0	1	6
	Blounts Law Dictionary Fol.	0	8	0
	Boltons Office of a Justice Fol.	1	0	0
L.	Brevia Judicialia Fol.	0	12	0
F.	Bendlowes Reports Fol.	0	6	0
	Bulstrodes Reports, 3 parts Fol.	1	4	0
	Bridgemans Reports Fol.	0	5	0
L.	Browns Entries Fol.	0	12	0
L.	Book of Entries the old Fol.	1	10	0
	Bacons Cases of Treason 4°	0	0	6
	—Charge 4°	0	0	6
	—Ordinances in Chancery 4°	0	0	6
	—Post Nati 4°	0	1	0
	—Elements Common Law 4°	0	2	0
	—Reading on the Stat. of Uses 4°	0	1	0
	—3 Speeches 4°	0	1	0
	Boons Exam. Legum Angliæ 4°	0	3	0
	Brownlows Declarations, 2 parts 4°	0	14	0
	—Juditial Writs 4°	0	3	0
	—Reports, 2 parts 4°	0	10	0
	Bagshaws Argum. in Parliament 4°	0	0	6
	Bridals View of the Laws of Eng. 8°	0	1	0
	Bagshaws Right of the Crown 8°	0	1	6
L.	Brevia Selecta 8°	0	1	6
F.	Bellews Richard II. 8	0	2	0
F.	Britton 8°	0	5	0
	Book of Oaths 8°	0	2	0
	C			
L.	Cooks Entries Fol.	3	0	0
*	—Comment on Littleton Fol.	0	18	0
*	—Magna Charta Fol.	0	14	0
*	—Pleas of the Crown Fol.	0	6	0
*	—Jurisdiction of Courts Fol.	0	8	0
F.	—Reports, 11. parts Fol.	3	0	0
	—Reports English, 13. parts Fol.	2	10	0
	—12. and 13. parts of Reports Fol.	0	8	0
	—Declarations Fol.	0	7	0
	—of Bails and Mainprizes 4°	0	0	6
	—Reading of Fines 4°	0	1	0
*	—Copy-holder 8°	0	1	6
	Cottons Records Fol.	1	0	0
	—Abstract of Recor 4°	0	0	6
*	Cowells Interpreter, with Manleys Additions } Folio.	0	8	0
	Customs of Normandy Fol.	1	0	0
*	Crooks Reports, 3 parts Fol.	2	5	0
	Collection of Ordin. & Decl. from March 42. to Decem. 46, Fol.	0	16	0
	Cooks Vindication of the Law 4°	0	1	0
	Calthrops Customs of London 4°	0	0	8
	—Copy-holder 4°	0	1	0
*	—Reports 8°	0	1	6
	Collect. of Remonstrances, Votes from 1641. to 1643. 4°	0	6	0
L.	Clarks Praxis in Curiis Ecclesiastic. 4°	0	6	0
L.	—Practice of the Admiralty 8°	0	1	0
	Callis Reading on Sewers 4°	0	4	0
	—Argument 4°	0	0	6
	Crook and Huttons Argument 4°	0	2	
*F	Cromptons Jurisdict. of Courts 4°	0	6	0
F.	Crompton & Fitzherberts Justice 4°	0	6	0
	Commission, with Instruct. for compounding for Idiots and Lun 4°	0	0	6
	Court of Request 4°	0	2	0
*	Compleat Clerk 4°	0	12	0
	Case of Ship-money 4°	0	0	8
	Clarendons Orders in Chancery 8°	0	1	
	Clark of Assize 8°	0	1	0
	City Law 8°	0	1	0
L.	Cowels Institutions 8°	0	2	0
	—The same in Engl. 8°	0	2	0
	Clarks Vade Mecum 8°	0	3	0
*	Clarks Guide, 4 parts 8°	0	5	0
*	Clarks Tutor 8°	0	1	6
	Careys Reports 8°	0	1	6
	Claytons Reports 8°	0	1	0
	Caryes Use of Pleadings 8°	0	1	6
*	Compleat Sollicitor 8°	0	3	6
*	Compleat Attourney 8°	0	3	0
	Charter of Rumny Marsh 8°	0	4	0
	Collins Justice 12°	0	1	0
	Carys Guide in Ecclesiast. Courts 12	0	1	0
	Court Marshals. with its Proceed 12°	0	1	0
*	Compleat Justice 12°	0	2	0
	Clarks Companion 24°	0	1	0
	D			
*	Daltons Office of Sheriffs Fol.	0	12	0
	—Sheriff Abr. 8°	0	3	0
*	—Justice Fol.	0	8	0
F	Dyers Reports with 2 Tables Fol.	0	18	0
	—Brograve, & Risdens Read. 4	0	1	6
F	—Abridgment 8°	0	2	0
	—The same in English 8°	0	2	0
*	Dugdales Orig. Juridiciales Fol.	0	14	0
F	Davis Reports Fol.	0	12	0
	—of Impositions. 8°	0	1	6
	—Ab. of Cooks Reports 12°	0	2	0
	Denshalls Reading of Fines 4°	0	0	6
	Dodridges Principalities of Wales 4°	0	1	0
	—English Lawyer 4°	0	2	6
	—Compl. Parson 4°	0	2	0
	—of Parliaments 8°	0	1	0
	Davenports Abr. of Cooks Lit. 8°	0	3	0
—	Doctor and Student 8°	0	2	0
	Doctor and Student Abridged 8°	0	1	0
	Derhams Manuel 8°	0	1	0
	E			
	Ephemeris Parliamentaria Fol.	0	6	0
	Elesmeres Post Nati 4°	0	1	0
	—on a Lord Chancellour 8°	0	1	0
	Elsynge of Parliaments 8°	0	2	0
	Edgars Charge 4°	0	0	6
	Exact Clerk 8°	0	1	0
	Exact Law-giver 8°	0	1	6
	Exact Constable 12°	0	1	0
	F			
F	Finches Law Fol.	0	8	0
	—in English 8°	0	3	0
	—Summary of the Law 8°	0	1	0
F	Fitzherberts Abridgement Fol.	1	5	0
F	—Quarto.	3	15	0
*F	—Natura Brevium 8°	0	5	0
*	—Nat. Brev. Eng. 8°	0	5	0
L	Fleta on the English Law 4°	0	2	0
	Fulbecks Parallel & Pandects 4°	0	18	0
	—Preparative 8°	0	1	6
	Fraunches Lawyers Logick 4°	0	3	0
	Freeholders Grand Inquest 4°	0	1	6
	Fillacers Office 8°	0	1	0
	Fleetwoods Justice 8°	0	1	0
	Forsters Lay-mans Lawyer 8°	0	2	0
F	Fidells Presidents 8°	0	2	6
*	Fortescu de Laudibus L. 8°	0	3	0
	G			
	Godboults Reports 4°	0	6	0
	Gouldsbroughs Reports 4°	0	3	6
	Glisson & Gulstons Ep. of the Law 8°	0	3	0
F	Gregories Moot-Book 8°	0	10	0
	—The same in Eng. 4°	0	10	0
*	Greenwood of Courts 8°	0	3	6
	Godolphin on the Admiralty 8°	0	2	0
	Grand Quest. on the House of Peers. 8°	0	8	0
L	Glanvil on the Law 8°	0	2	0
	H			
	Huttons Reports Fol.	0	7	0
	Hetleys Reports Fol.	0	5	0
*	Hobarts Reports Fol.	0	10	0
	Herns Pleader Fol.	0	18	0
	—Law of Conveyances 8°	0	2	0
	—Moddern Assurancer 8°	0	2	6
*	—Law of Charitable Uses 8°	0	2	0
	—Reading on Sewers 4°	0	0	6
	Hughes Grand Abridge. 3 parts 4°	2	10	0
	—Abridge. of Acts & Ordin. 4°	0	8	0
	—Original Writts 4°	0	3	6
	—Abr. of Crooks 3 Rep. 8°	0	6	0
	—Abr. Acts 16,17,18. Car. I. and 12, 13, 14, 15. CAR. II. 8°	0	2	6
	—Abr. of Moors Reports 8°	0	2	6
*	—Parsons Law 8°	0	2	0
	Huntley & Kingleys Arguments 4°	0	1	0
	Hakewels Liberty of the Subject 4°	0	1	0
	—manner of pass. Bills in P. 8°	0	1	0
*	—Of Parliaments 8°	0	2	0
F	Hornes Mirrour of Justice 8°	0	2	0
	—The same in English 8°	0	2	0
	Hawkes Grounds of the Law 8°	0	4	0
	Historical discourse of Parliam. 8°	0	1	0
	Heydons Idea of the Law 8°	0	1	6
	J			
F	Jenkins Reports Fol.	0	9	0
	—of Courts 8°	0	1	0
	—Liberty of the Subject 12°	0	1	0
	Justice Restored 12°	0	1	0
	Irelands Abr. of Cooks 11 Voll. 8°	0	2	6
	Justice Revived 8°	0	1	6
	Institutions or Grounds of Law 8°	0	1	0
	Judgements in the Upper Bench 8°	0	2	6
	Instructions for Jury-men 8°	0	1	6
	K			
*F	Kelleweys Rep., with Dallison Fol.	0	14	0
*F	Kitchin of Courts 8°	0	4	0
*	—The same in Engl. 8°	0	4	0
	L			
F	Latches Reports Fol.	0	7	0
	Lanes Reports Fol.	0	4	6
	Leys Reports Fol.	0	4	0
	Leonards Reports, 3 parts Fol.	1	4	0
L	Lambert of the Laws of Engl. Fol.	0	12	0
*	—Duty of Constables 12°	0	1	0
	—of Courts 8°	0	1	6
*	—Perambulation of Kent 8°	0	7	0
*	—Justice 8°	0	7	0
L,	Linwoods Constitutions Fol.	1	5	0
	Layers Office & Duty of Constables 8°	0	1	0
	Ley of Wards and Liveries 8°	0	1	0
—	Leighs Law Terms 8	0	1	6
	Legis Fluvius 8°	0	1	0
	Littletons Tenures Fr. & Eng. 12°	0	2	6
F,	—Vicesimo Quarto.	0	2	6
	M			
F	Moores Reports Fol.	1	15	0
*	Manwoods Forest Laws 4°	0	6	0
	Moyles Entries 4°	0	3	0
	Method of passing Bills in Parliam. 4°	0	0	6
	Marches Reports 4°	0	4	0
	—Actions for Slander 2 Parts 8°	0	2	6
	—Amicus Reipublicæ 8°	0	1	0
*	Meritons Guide for Constables 12°	0	1	6
*	—Landlords Law 12°	0	1	6
	—of Wills and Testaments 12°	0	1	6
	N			
	Noyes Reports Fol.	0	5	0
	—Maxims of the Law 8°	0	1	6
	—Compleat Lawyer 8°	0	1	0
	Nusances, with Judges Resolution 4°	0	0	6
L	Novæ Narrationes, with Articul. 8°	0	4	0
	O			
	Olivers Ordinances Fol.	0	6	0
	Owens Reports Fol.	0	5	0
	Orders for the Poor 4°	0	0	6
F	Old Natura Brevium 8°	0	2	0
	Orders of a Court Leet, & C. Baron 8°	0	0	6
	P			
*	Pultons Stat. at large. Fol.	2	10	0
	—de Pace Fol.	0	10	0
	—Abr. of Stat. Fol.	0	12	0
	—Abr. of P. Statutes 4°	0	3	6
F	Plowdens Rep. 2 parts, 3 Tables Fol.	1	15	0
F	—Queries 8°	0	2	6
	—Queries English 8°	0	2	0
F	—Abridged 8°	0	2	0
	—The same in English 8°	0	2	0
	Pophams Reports Fol.	0	7	0
	Pryns Animad. on Cooks 4. Inst. Fol.	0	12	0
	—Parliamentary Writts, 4 Vol. 4°	1	0	0
	Practice and Priviledges of Parl. 4°	0	0	6
	Practice of the Court of Com. Ple. 4°	0	0	6
	Perfect Conveyancer 4°	0	5	0
	Parsons Ans. to Cooks 5th Report 4°	0	8	0
	Powell of Courts 4°	0	2	6
	—Reportery of Records 4°	0	2	0
	—Direct. to search Records 4°	0	2	0
*	—Attourney Academy 4°	0	3	6
	—Attourneys Almanack 4°	0	1	0
	Practice of the Exchequer 8°	0	1	0
	Practice of Chancery 8°	0	1	6
F	Perkins 8°	0	2	0
	—The same in English 8°	0	2	0
	—Vicesimo Quarto.	0	2	0
	Presidents or Instruments 8°	0	1	6
	Pages Jus Fratrum 8°	0	1	6
	Prothonotaries Fees, & Fees in Ch. 8°	0	1	0
	Phillips Studij Legalis 12	0	1	6
	—Principles of Law 12°	0	1	0
	Practica Walliæ 12°	0	1	6
	R			
F	Rolls Abridgement of the Law Fol.	2	0	0
L	Ryleys Records of the Tower Fol.	0	18	0
L	Register of Writs Fol.	1	5	0
L	Rastals Entries Fol.	3	0	0
	—Stat. from M. C. to 16 Jac. Fol.	1	10	0
	—Abr. of the Stat. to 7 Jac. Fol.	0	12	0
	Rights of the Kingdom 4°	0	8	0
	Rights of the People 8°	0	1	0
	Rules & Orders in the Upper Bench, Com. Ple. & Chanc. made 1654.	0	2	6
	Ridleys View of Civil Law 8°	0	3	6
	S			
F	Stathams Abr. Fol.	1	15	0
	Shepheards Epitome Fol.	1	15	0
	—Law of Common Assurances Fol.	0	14	0
	—Practical Counsellour Fol.	0	12	0
	—Actions of the Case for Words Fol.	0	6	0
	—Actions of the Case for Deeds. Fol.	0	8	0
	—Marrow of Law, 2 parts 4°	0	10	0
	—Touch-Stone 4°	0	6	0
	—President of Presidents 4	0	3	6
*	—Duty of a Constable 8°	0	1	6
	—Court-keepers Guide 8°	0	1	6
	—Guide for a Justice 8°	0	3	6
	—Clarks Cabinet 8°	0	1	0
	—Clark of the Market 8°	0	1	0
	—Of Corporations 8°	0	1	0
	—Survey of Justice 12°	0	1	4
	—Proposals 8°	0	1	6
	—Of County Judicatures 8°	0	1	0
	—Of Tythes 12°	0	1	
	—View of the Laws 12°	0	1	
*L	Spelmans Glossary Fol.	2	0	
	Stiles Reports Fol.	0	10	
*	—Pract. Register 8°	0	3	
	Stat. Ed. 2. to the 11. Jacob. Irish. Fol.	0	18	
	Scobells Collection of Acts Fol.	0	16	
L	Skenes Scotch Laws Fol.	0	12	
	The same in Scotch Fol.	0	12	
	—De significat Verborum 4°	0	2	
L	Seldens Mare Clausum Fol.	0	12	
	—The same in English Fol.	0	12	
	—History of Tythes 4°	0	8	
	—Of Barronage. 8°	0	1	
	Sherman on Estates Tayle 4°	0	0	
	Special Law Cases 4°	0	2	
	S. Johns Argument 4°	0	0	
	Star-chamber Cases 4°	0	0	
*F	Stamfords Pleas of the Crown 4°	0	6	
	Somner of Gavell Kinde 4°	0	2	
	Smalls Declarations 4°	0	3	
	Seldens History of Tythes 4°	0	8	
*	Swinbourn of Wills 4°	0	10	
	Sharrock on Linwood 12°	0	6	
	Stones Reading of Bankrupts 8°	0	1	
	Statute of Bankrupts, by T. B. 8°	0	1	6
	Statuta Vetera & Recentiora 8°	0	1	
—	Smiths Common-wealth of Eng. 12°	0	1	6
	Sheriffs Practice in London 12°	0	1	
	T			
L	Thesaurus Brevium Fol.	0	6	0
	Tenures of Ireland Fol.	0	8	0
LF	Townesends Tables Fol.	0	12	0
	Taylor of Gavel Kinde 4°	0	3	0
	Thorps Charge 4°	0	0	6
	Tything Table 4°	0	0	6
F	Trotmans Ab. Cooks 11 Reports 8°	0	4	6
	Tothills Transactions in Chancery 8°	0	1	6
	Tryals Per Pais 8°	0	1	6
*	Terms of the Law 8°	0	4	6
	Topicks of the Law 8°	0	1	0
F	Theloals Digest. of Writts 8°	0	8	0
	Tennants Law 12°	0	1	0
	V			
	Vernons Consid. in Exchequer 8°	0	1	0
	W			
	Wingats Maxims Fol.	0	14	0
*	—Ab. Statutes 8°	0	6	0
*	—Body of the Law 8°	0	1	6
	—Statut. Pacis 12°	0	2	0
	Waterhouse on Fortescue Fol.	0	16	0
*	Winches Reports Fol.	0	5	0
	Wests Presidents 2 Parts 4°	0	14	0
	Womans Lawyer 4°	0	4	0
	Wisemans Law of Laws 4°	0	2	6
	White on the Sacred Law °	0	1	6
	Welwoods Abridge. of Sea Laws 8°	0	1	6
*	Wentworths Executors Office 8°	0	2	0
	Wilkinsons Office of a Sheriff 8°	0	2	6
	Y			
F	Yelvertons Reports Fol.	0	8	0
	Youngs Vade Mecum 12°	0	1	0
	Z			
	Zouch on the Admiralty 8°	0	2	0

Year Books.

			l.	s.	d.
	EDW. III. 1 part.	15 l.	0	00	0
	EDW. III. 2 part.		0	00	0
	Quadragesimes		0	00	0
	Book of Assizes		0	00	0
	HEN. IV. & V.		0	00	0
	HEN. VI. 1 part.		0	00	0
	HEN. VI. 2 part		0	00	0
*	EDW. IV.		0	00	0
	Long Quinto.		0	00	0
	HEN VII.		0	00	0

These Ten Volumes of Year Books are intended shortly to be Re-printed, with a Table to the whole, and Sold for about halfe the present Price, by way of Subscription.

Collected by Thomas Basset Bookseller, at the George near Cliffords Inne, in Fleet-street, 1673.

3. Private Libraries

At one time it was supposed that there were no lawyers in seventeenth-century New England because there were no reports printed here. This is a naive view of the profession, which had carried out its responsibilities in England for centuries without print; and an overly restrictive view of the law, as the possession of a professional caste. The Colony provided for a public record in MS. of important cases, an example of which survives in the Pynchon diary, but in general the law was administered by lay judges, many of whom would have had great trouble understanding the professional literature. The Colony printed statutes in a form easily intelligible by laymen, and a few professionals like Thomas Lechford in Boston easily engrossed most of the remaining business (Roger North records that a single serjeant handled the entire business of a seventeenth-century English circuit, which represents a roughly equivalent population). Any books they needed, moreover, were easily supplied from England.

THOMAS BASSET *An exact catalogue of the common & statute law books of this realm, and some others relating thereunto* [London] : T. Basset, 1672.
> This is one of the first specialized bookseller's catalogues; the number of titles shows why.

RICHARD BELLINGHAM (owner) *Tractatus de legibus & consuetudinibus regni Angliae* / Ralph de Glanville [London] : T. Wright, 1604; bound with *Dialogus de fundamentis legum Angliae et de conscientiae* ["Doctor & Student"] / Christopher Saint German [London] : T. Wright, 1604.
> Bellingham (ca. 1592–1672) had been a professional lawyer in England, where he was Recorder of Boston. He was one of the Massachusetts Bay patentees, and became Governor of the Colony in 1665. According to the DAB, "his peculiar will . . . produced litigation lasting over 100 years." *O si sic omnes!*

NICHOLAS MOREY (owner) *The compleat solicitor* London : Assigns of R. and E. Atkyns, for J. Cotterell and F. Collins, 1683.
> Morey has entered notes of some cases at Plymouth, 1722 on the fly-leaf at back. This is the sole record of his existence, though the Morey family is attested in Plymouth.

ELISHA COOKE (owner) *A new survey of the justice of peace his office* / William Sheppard London : J.S., 1659; with *Littletons Tenures in English* London: Co. of Stationers, 1612.
> Books from the library of Elisha Cooke (1678–1737) are among the glories of Harvard College Library, as this exhibition makes clear. A physician and statesman, he was appointed to the Court of Common Pleas in Suffolk County, 1731. "Cooke and his father inherited independent traditions of the old colony and transmitted them to the era of Adams and Otis" (DAB); indeed, the puzzling word *caucus* has been derived by corruption from "Cooke's house."

JEREMIAH GRIDLEY (owner) *The judges' resolution upon the several statutes concerning bankrupts* / George Billinghurst London : For H. Twyford, 1676.
> Gridley (1702–1767), Attorney General of the Province in the last year of his life, "a broad-minded, cultivated man, an able lawyer averse to technicalities, and cared little for wealth" (DAB). He presented John Adams to the Bar in 1758.

JOSIAH COTTON (owner) *The Book of the general laws of the inhabitants of . . . New-Plimouth* Boston : S. Green, 1685.
> With a list of a purchase of this and some English law books, 8 May 1718, on the front fly-leaf. Josiah Cotton (1680–1756) was a schoolmaster and Indian missionary, who also held a

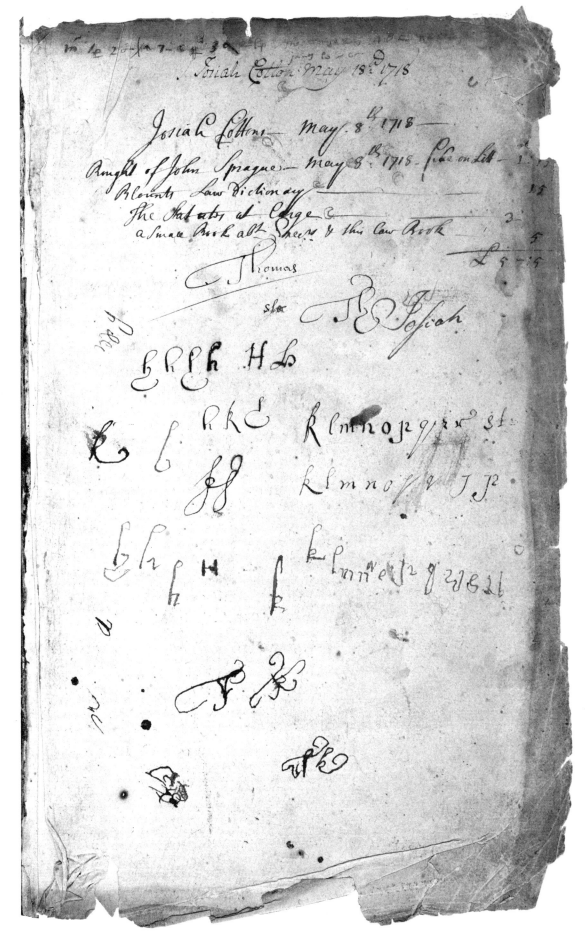

Josiah Cotton purchases *Coke on Littleton*, Blount's *Law Dictionary*, the *Laws* of New Plymouth and a "small Book ab[ou]t Exec[uto]rs."

variety of legal offices from 1713, serving as Justice of the Inferior Court, 1721–1739. A busy man, with fourteen children and a farm in addition to his law business, he still had time for his religious duties. Sibley and Shipton (Class of 1698) note, "He traveled constantly over Plymouth Colony, preaching on the average twenty Sundays a year" for half a century. Clergymen like Cotton were the chief dealers in books in early New England, as John Dunton observed in 1705.

4. Blank Forms

MASSACHUSETTS (Colony) *The oath of a freeman* / introd. by L.C. Wroth   New York : Press of the Wooly Whale, 1939.
> The most famous blank form of all time. No printed copy of this, the first production of the Cambridge Press, survives, but there are two MS. drafts, by Governor Winthrop and Thomas Dudley, and the text was reprinted in the 1648 *Laws*. It is thus a favorite object of forgery; most forgeries look something like this scholarly reprint, but no one really knows what the original looked like, though the layout may have resembled that of the London oaths. The failure of the oath to recognize the King's sovereignty was one cause of the revocation of the Colony Charter in 1685.

LONDON, Eng.   *The oath of euery free-man of the City of London*   [London] : R. Young, [after 1625]

LONDON, Eng.   *The oath of every free-man of the City of London*   [London] : J. Flesher, [1653?]

SUFFOLK COUNTY COURT   *Decree by Isaac Addington, in the matter of the Last will and testament of Ebenezer Clapp*, 17 Aug. 1712.

JOSEPH BELCHER   *Mortgage of land to John Clarke, Adam Winthrop, Elisha Cooke and Samuel Thaxter*, 6 Feb. 1721/22.
> Witnessed by the printer of the form, Bartholomew Green; an indenture, cut at the top to match a duplicate copy (these indentations give it its name). A sheepskin might have been large enough to produce two copies, but paper wasn't, and presumably the matching copy was overlapped before the wavy cut was made.

5. Lay Judges

SIMON BRADSTREET   *Memoires*, 1675 (with facsimile, enlarged)
> The case of the unspeakable Jonathan Rogers, an Anabaptist who (not at all to Bradstreet's surprise) had sex with a negro woman (whom he then tried to poison), an English maid, Indian squaws, a certain Mr. Sherwood, mares, cows, goats, sheep, sows, a bitch, and a tame moose, all of which he "boasted of" to his wife, but could not be convicted of his multiple capital offences, because her evidence was legally inadmissible.

WILLIAM PYNCHON *Diary*, 1639–1650.
> Mr. Pynchon reads the newly printed *Lauues and libertyes* aloud in court; so the sheriff would "publish" the English statutes aloud in the county market. The practise defines sales of the 1648 *Laws* at about thirty copies, one for each township. Similarly the practise of "lining out a psalm" limited absolute demand to one psalm book a congregation. But the Founders were far-sighted men: they printed 600 copies of the 1648 *Laws* and 1700 of the Bay Psalm Book.

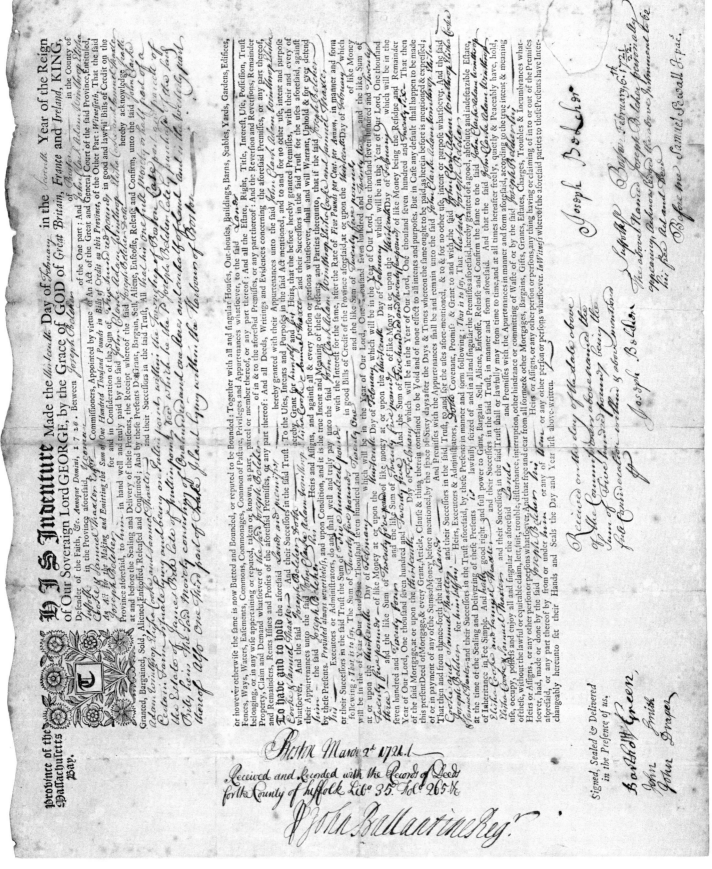

JOSEPH BELCHER *Mortgage*, 6 Feb. 1722

The Oath of euery Free-man of the Citie of LONDON.

Ee ſhall ſweare, that yee ſhall be good and true to our Soueraign Lord King Charles, & to the heires of our ſaid Soueraigne Lord the King. Obeyſant and obedient yee ſhall be to the Maior and Miniſters of this City. The Franchiſes and Cuſtomes thereof ye ſhall maintaine, and this City kéepe harmleſſe in that that in you is. Ye ſhall be Contributory to all manner of charges within this City, as Summons, Watches, Contributions, Taxes, Tallages, Lot and Scot, and to all other charges, bearing your part as a Frée-man ought to doe Ye ſhall colour no Forraigne goods, vnder or in your name, whereby the King or this City might or may loſe their cuſtomes or aduantages. Ye ſhall know no Forraigner to buy or ſell any Merchandize, with any other forraigner within this City or franchiſe thereof, but ye ſhall warne the Chamberlaine thereof, or ſome miniſter of the Chamber. Ye ſhall implead or ſue no Frée-man out of this City, whiles ye may haue right and law within the ſame City. Ye ſhall take none Apprentiſe, but if he be Frée-borne (that is to ſay) no bondmans ſon, nor the childe of any Alien, and for no leſſe terme than for ſeuen yéeres, without fraud or deceit: and within the firſt yéere yee ſhall cauſe him to be enrolled, or elſe pay ſuch fine as ſhalbe reaſonably impoſed vpon you for omitting the ſame. And after his termes end, within conuenient time (being required) ye ſhal make him frée of this City, if he haue well and truly ſerued you. Ye ſhall alſo kéepe the Kings peace in your owne perſon Ye ſhall know no gatherings, conuenticles, nor conſpiracies made againſt the Kings Peace, but ye ſhall warne the Maior thereof, or let it to your power. All theſe points and articles ye ſhal well and truly kéep, according to the lawes & cuſtomes of this City, to your power. So God you helpe. God ſaue the King.

Printed by Robert Young, Printer to this Honourable City.

May. 25. 1675. Jno. Rogers of
N: London aged aboute 28 (& not
many months before turnd a prond
Anabaptist) was arraigned at Hartfd
at ye Court of Assistants upon tryall
of his life. His crimes wr.
1. for fornication, with a Negro, an English
   maid, & Indean Squaw.
2. Attempt of murder, giveing rats-
   bane to ye negroe woman by who
   he hay a bastard yet liveing.
3. For Sodomy with one Sherwood.
4. For Bestiality. with Mares, Cowes,
   goates, sheep, Sowes, a bitch, and
   a Tame moose yt Major winthrop
   had Eere in ye Town.
The Testimony agst him was -his
own wife (a prudent sober young
woman) to who he told it all wth
his own mouth, not in trouble of
mind, but in a boasting manner of
free grace, yt he was pardoned: This
was much about ye time he fell into
yt cursed opinion of Anabaptisme. His
wife advised wth some of ye magistr &
Elders about her revealing of it,
weh she advised to.
There ware very many Testimonies
by way of Circumste, to confirm his
wives testimony.
The Grandjury could not legally
find him guilty, & so he had
his Goal-deliuery. He would not
deny his crimes but stood vpon legall
evid. the whole bench, and all
sober persons judge him guilty.
He is now at liberty but I beleiue
he will not escape gods Judgmt, tho:
he has mans. —

SIMON BRADSTREET *Memoires*

MASSACHUSETTS (Colony) GENERAL COURT *Summons in a trial for witchcraft,* 13 May 1680.
Ransacking two counties for twelve good men and true (two each from Charlestown, Watertown, Cambridge and Dorchester, and five from Boston); out west, in thinly settled Agawam, Pynchon made do with panels of six.

COTTON MATHER *The wonders of the invisible world* Boston : B. Harris, 1693 [i.e. 1692]
Witchcraft, in the shtetl of Salem Village (now Danvers, though Salem has taken over the glory). There is no literature of trials in seventeenth-century New England — it is more or less subsumed in journalism like this, the official defense of the trial; the English literature for the most part dates from the period of the Popish Plot.

WILLIAM HANNUM, et al. *Copy, attested by Elizur Holyoke of Springfield, of depositions against Mary Parson for witchcraft,* 11 Aug. 1656.
The case began before William Pynchon.

HENRY CARE *English liberties* London : G. Larkin for B. Harris, [1680?].
This treatise, produced at the height of the Popish Plot by a rabid Whig printer, became an American classic, reprinted down to the Revolution.

NICHOLAS BOONE *The constables pocket-book* Boston : E. Phillips, 1710.
A typical early American treatise; wholly practical, and non-professional, written by a printer who knew what would sell.

SAMUEL GREEN *Writ directing the marshal of Essex Co. to attach the goods or persons of Philip Nelson and Jeremiah Jewitt,* 7 Mar. 1664.
The Harvard College printer also served as Clerk of the Writs of Middlesex County, from 1652.

6. Legislation

JOHN COTTON *An abstract or* [sic] *the lavves of Nevv England, as they are novv established* London : F. Coules and W. Ley, 1641.
Extracted from an experimental code of 1636, usually known as "Moses his Judicialls." Despite the t.-p., it was never "established." The Biblical inspiration is obvious, but can be overemphasized; more interesting is the attempt to distribute land equitably and limit its accumulation — paralleling similar legislative proposals of the time in England.

NATHANIEL WARD *The capitall lawes of New-England* London : B. Allen, 1643.
Extracted from Ward's "Body of liberties," a trial code in force 1642–45. More than any other image, this is responsible for the popular belief that early Massachusetts was governed by the Torah, "under God." The *Capital laws* were also cumulated in the *Lauues and libertyes* (1648), which superseded most of Ward's code. Though the imposition of capital punishment for adultery and even for striking one's parents seems cruelly reactionary, it anticipates trends in eighteenth-century English law. As in most revolutionary codes, the message is one of social solidarity against deviance.

An estimated 2,000 copies were printed, none of which survive; only two copies remain of this London reprint, one in the British Library, and this copy, which Harvard bought from Lincoln Cathedral Library in 1955. The New England printing sold slowly: as late as 1674, the Watertown Meeting resolved that "Each man heave in his house a Coppy," to be paid for out of the rates (D.G. Allen, *In English Ways* [Chapel Hill: Univ. of North Carolina Press, 1981], p. 219–20). They must mean copies of the first edition, so that the printer's stock was depleted by less than 65 copies a year, on an average.

Sold alfo by *Richard Chifwel,*

NEw-*England's Memorial*; or a Relation of the moft memorable and Remarkable Paffages of the Providence of God manifefted to the Planters of *New-England* in *America*, with fpecial Reference to the Colony of *New-Plimouth.* By *Nathanael Morton*, Secretary to the Court for the Jurifdiction of *New-Plimouth*; in *quarto.*

God's Call to his People to turn unto Him, together with his Promife to turn unto them ; opened and applied in two Sermons at two publick Fafting-days appointed by Authority. By *John Davenport*, Paftor of a Church of Chrift at *Bofton* in *New-England* ; in *quarto.*

Both printed at Cambridge *in New-England.*

Cambridg Concordance, By S. *Newman,* in *fol.* 1672.
Caryl on *Job* compleat, in twelve Volumns. *quarto.*
Burroughs Jewel of Contentment. *quarto.*
Difcription and Hiftory of the Future State of *Europe,* to 1700. *quart.*
Lyford's Difcovery of Errors and Herefies. *quart.*
Dr. *Jacomb's* Sermons on *Rom.* 8. in *quart.*
Culverwels Difcourfe of the Light of Nature. *quart.*
Gouges Word to Saints and Sinners. *octavo.*
Bryans Intereft and Duty of Believers. *octav.*
Difcourfe of the Nature,Ends,and Difference of the two Covenants.*oct.*
Powels Concordance to the Bible; *octav.*
Rolls Anfwer to the Friendly Debate. *oct.*
Apology for the Nonconformifts. *oct.*
Davenports Power of Congregational Churches. *oct.*
Hardcaftles Chriftian Geography and Arithmetick. *oct.*
Mathers Sermons about Converfion. *oct.*
Dyers Work ; *duodec.*
Abbots Young mans Warning-piece. *duod.*
New England Pfalms. *duod.*
Shepherds found Believer. *oct.*
Ign. Fullers Sermons of Peace and Holinefs. *oct.*
Friendly Debate, 1ft and 2d part.
Buckler of State and Juftice againft *France's* Defign of Univerfal Monarchy. *oct.*
Free Conference touching the prefent State of England at home and abroad, in order to the defigns of *France. oct.*
Lord *Barkleys* Hiftorical Applications. *oct.*
The Jefuits Intrigues; *quart.*

MASSACHUSETTS (Colony) *The book of the general lavves and libertyes concerning the inhabitants of the Massachusets* Cambridge : [S. Green], 1660.
 The second cumulation (the first, 1648, survives in a unique copy, now in the Huntington Library). The alphabetical arrangement by topic meets the needs of lay judges. It is the normal arrangement for J.P. manuals, for example, one of which, Pulton's *De Pace,*

THE GENERAL
LAWS
AND
LIBERTIES
OF THE
Massachusets Colony
IN
New-England,

Revised and Reprinted,

By Order of the General Court holden at *BOSTON*,
May 15th, 1672.

Edward Rawson, Secr.

Whosoever therefore resisteth the Power, resisteth the Ordinance of God ; and they that resist, receive to themselves Damnation. Rom. 13. 2.

Cambridge in *New-England*,

Printed by *Samuel Green*, for *John Usher* of *Boston*, and to be sold by *Richard Chiswel*, at the Rose and Crown in St. *Paul's* Church-yard, *London*, 1675.

provided the topical scheme and digest of English statutes for the first edition. It was updated by supplements until the third cumulation, in 1672, and paid for out of the county rates. This is probably an official copy, for it is bound in black calf, stamped with the royal arms; the gift of Justice Joseph Story, 1837. The t.-p. is wanting, supplied in a modern facsimile.

MASSACHUSETTS (Colony) GENERAL COURT   *A declaration of the General Court of the Massachusets holden at Boston in New England, October 18. 1659, concerning the execution of two Quakers*   Reprinted in London, 1659.

On 8 April 1659, William Robinson was travelling between Newport, R.I. and Daniel Gould's house, when he heard God's voice commanding him "to pass to the Town of Boston, *my life to lay down in his Will.*" He and his companions Marmaduke Stephenson and Mary Dyer accordingly went, and were convicted of heresy, whipped for protesting their innocence, and sentenced to banishment on pain of death, in August 1659. They continued to preach the doctrine of Christ in the Puritan darkness, and the men were duly hanged, on 27 October, proclaiming God's judgment on the Colony. Contrary to the allegations of this broadside, Mary Dyer refused the Court's mercy, and had to be removed from the scaffold by force.

The original text of the Court's defense against divine wrath and human criticism survives in two English reprints only. The law was probably *ultra vires*, but the Quakers did not appeal to England, because they did not recognize their authority either. The English editions survived because the Court's real audience was the mother country; the Massachusetts printing was *pro forma*.

MASSACHUSETTS (Colony)   *The general laws and liberties of Massachusetts Colony,* Revised and re-printed   Cambridge : S. Green for J. Usher of Boston, 1672. Autographed "Arthur Mason his book 1675," showing the female, Cambridge press version of the Colony seal, engraved by John Foster. This version reflects its original model, the seal of the University of Cambridge (in facsimile).

Note the imprint: this is the first commercially distributed collection, financed by Usher, who secured his property with a colonial patent for seven years; the first American copyright. The wonderful thing about laws, from a printer's point of view, is that they are constantly revised and growing, unlike works of literature,which have no built-in obsolescence.

MASSACHUSETTS (Colony)   *The general laws and liberties of the Massachusetts Colony in New England*   Cambridge : S. Green for J. Usher, and sold by R. Chiswell . . . London, 1675. American-printed sheets, reissued in London with a cancel t.-p. and leaf of advertisements for Chiswell's publications; this is the first time an English publisher purchases American printing, instead of pirating it.

A
DECLARATION
OF THE
GENERAL COURT
OF THE
MASSACHVSETS

Holden at *Boston* in *New-England*, October 18. 1659. Concerning
The execution of two Quakers.

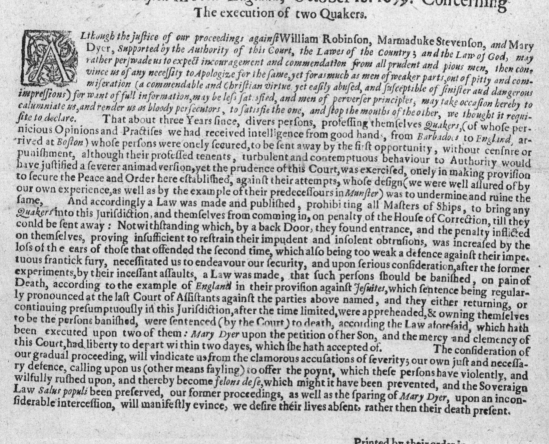

Lthough the justice of our proceedings against William Robinson, Marmaduke Stevenson, and Mary Dyer, *Supported by the Authority of this Court, the Lawes of the Country; and the Law of God, may rather perswade us to expect incouragement and commendation from all prudent and pious men, then convince us of any necessity to Apologize for the same,* yet forasmuch as men of weaker parts, out of pitty and commiseration (a commendable and Christian virtue, yet easily abused, and susceptible of sinister aud dangerous impressions) for want of full information, may be less satisfied, and men of perverser principles, may take occasion hereby to calumniate us, and render us as bloody persecutors, to satisfie the one, and stop the mouths of the other, we thought it requisite to declare. That about three Years since, divers persons, professing themselves *Quakers,* (of whose pernicious Opinions and Practises we had received intelligence from good hands, from *Barbadoes* to *England,* arrived at *Boston*) whose persons were onely secured, to be sent away by the first opportunity, without censure or punishment, although their professed tenents, turbulent and contemptuous behaviour to Authority would have justified a severer animadversion, yet the prudence of this Court, was exercised, onely in making provision to secure the Peace and Order here established, against their attempts, whose design (we were well assured of by our own experience, as well as by the example of their predecessours in *Munster*) was to undermine and ruine the same, And accordingly a Law was made and published, prohibiting all Masters of Ships, to bring any *Quakers* into this Jurisdiction, and themselves from comming in, on penalty of the House of Correction, till they could be sent away : Notwithstanding which, by a back Door, they found entrance, and the penalty inflicted on themselves, proving insufficient to restrain their impudent and insolent obtrusions, was increased by the loss of the ears of those that offended the second time, which also being too weak a defence against their impetuous frantick fury, necessitated us to endeavour our security, and upon serious consideration, after the former experiments, by their incessant assaults, a Law was made, that such persons should be banished, on pain of Death, according to the example of *England* in their provision against *Jesuites,* which sentence being regularly pronounced at the last Court of Assistants against the parties above named, and they either returning, or continuing presumptuously in this Jurisdiction, after the time limited, were apprehended, & owning themselves to be the persons banished, were sentenced (by the Court) to death, according the Law aforesaid, which hath been executed upon two of them : *Mary Dyer* upon the petition of her Son, and the mercy and clemency of this Court, had liberty to depart within two dayes, which she hath accepted of. The consideration of our gradual proceeding, will vindicate us from the clamorous accusations of severity; our own just and necessary defence, calling upon us (other means fayling) to offer the poynt, which these persons have violently, and wilfully rushed upon, and thereby become *felons de se,* which might it have been prevented, and the Soveraign Law *Salus populi* been preserved, our former proceedings, as well as the sparing of *Mary Dyer,* upon an inconsiderable intercession, will manifestly evince, we desire their lives absent, rather then their death present.

Reprinted in *London,* 1659

Printed by their order in

NEW-ENGLAND.

Edward Rawson, Secretary.

FINIS.

THE DAY-GREEN ACCOUNTS

The first press in Cambridge was the property of Elizabeth Glover, a wealthy widow, who managed it from her arrival in 1638 to her death in 1643,[1] when it became the responsibility of her second husband Henry Dunster, president of Harvard and unhappy guardian of her expensive children. He ran the press until the paper was nearly exhausted in 1649, when he leased it to Samuel Green at 10/0 a sheet. In 1654, Dunster retired from the presidency on charges of antipaedobaptism, sold the press to Harvard, and left Cambridge.[2]

He had been unable to secure court approval of his guardianship, and in 1656 the Glover heirs sued for an accounting. The documents produced in this controversy, now in the Harvard Archives, are our main source for the early history of the press. The most important are 1) an affidavit by Steven Day stating that Mrs. Glover brought £60 of paper with her and "sold" £6 — presumably in unprinted form — before her death; 2) a rough account (allowed in an initial action by the Glovers) for £192 of "profits" realized by the press, drawn up by Steven Day and his successor, Samuel Green; and finally 3) the determination by the Middlesex bench on final review of the Glover claims and Dunster's counterclaims.

The Day-Green accounts are a confused, *ex parte* document, which cannot be taken at face value. Steven Day was so obviously hostile that President Dunster prayed for his soul in open court. He and Green overstate Dunster's profits (about which they could have known little) by assuming that he sold every sheet he printed for hard cash; whereas it is clear that many copies were still unsold in 1656, and Dunster's usual receipts were in "country pay," i.e. corn or wheat, whose value, moreover, had fluctuated wildly in the 1640's.[3] And finally, the accounts ignore Dunster's actual responsiblities, charging him for items printed in his wife's lifetime, and for items that had been printed on orders of the General Court.

The Middlesex Court's final determination is our only hope for controlling these distortions. The atmosphere was tense, and Justice Bellingham left the court room in a huff; but we can infer a kind of rough justice. The court disallowed all "profits" but £26 10s., most of which must be attributed to items that certainly sold, such as the almanacs and theses (£21 8s. 9d. in the accounts). They charged Dunster £50 for "press and paper." The press is elsewhere valued at £20, so that Dunster was held accountable for 120 reams of paper at the standard value of 5/0 used in accounts. Most of this is chargeable to the 116 reams used, according to Day and Green, for the Bay Psalm Book. Dunster was not charged for government printing, then.

The accounts include trial as well as final calculations, and compute expenses now in reams of paper, now in pounds. Day and Green were directly responsible for every sheet that passed through their hands, and any errors were easily controlled by looking at what was left in the warehouse. I have therefore converted all their figures to reams of paper, which is at least a stable "currency" compared to "country pay." The printers' fanciful opinions on President Dunster's profits are ignored. The period covered by the accounts is also obscure, at both ends. I assume that they end when Mrs. Glover's 240 reams were finally printed off, in 1653 or 4, and begin when Steven Day's indenture terminated, in 1640. This would explain why he charges for only 33 of the 37 sheets in the Bay Psalm Book: the rest were under contract. I have had to estimate some lost items, but they amount to only 8–9 reams in all: the Freeman's oath, the *Capital laws*, Davenport's *Catechism*, and Eliot's *Indian primer*. A ream is here taken as 480 sheets.

NOTES:

1. Henry protested that "he never knew any estate was in law his" during his marriage (Jeremiah Chaplin, *Life of Henry Dunster* [Boston, 1872], p. 212). The Colony paid President and Mrs. Dunster separately for the *Capital laws*, as S.E. Morison observes (*The Founding of Harvard College* [Cambridge: Harvard Univ. Press, 1935], p. 346, n. 5).

2. Winship, *Cambridge press*, p. 127; Winship speculates that Dunster mingled his (Harvard's) property with the Glover estate, but there is absolutely no evidence for the conjecture.

3. The value of wheat varied from 2/6 to 4/0 a bushel between 1640 and 1645; the 1654 Supplement to the *Laws* was paid "in wheat" (Winship, *Cambridge press*, p. 122).

PAPER ACCOUNTS, 1638–1653
Day-Green Press

	(reams)	
	Dr.	Cr.
Per ELIZABETH GLOVER (d. 1643)		
Steven and Matthew Day, printers: indentured, 1638–39; paid		
£1 a sheet thereafter; Steven quit ca. 1643.		
Imported by Elizabeth Glover, 1638		240
[*Freeman's oath* (1639)		
1/4 sh.: 2000 copies?]	1	
[*Psalms* (1640)		
4 sh., 4to: A–D⁴]		

———————————————————Accounts begin———————————————————

33 sh., 4to: E–V⁴, W⁴, X–L1⁴, *–***⁴ /		
1700 copies = [14+] + 116+ reams	131	
Capital laws (1642)		
1/2 sh.: [2000 copies?]		
Spelling book (1642?)		
[3 sh.?; 600 copies?]	6–7	
Almanacs for 1640–44		
1 sh.: [5 × 180 copies?]		
Harvard *Theses*, 1642–43		
1 sh.: [2 × 60 copies?]	2½	
Sold by Elizabeth Glover, 1638–43	24	
TOTAL	164–5½	240

Per HENRY DUNSTER		
Matthew Day, printer (d. 1649)		
From Glover account, 1643		74–5½
Narragansetts (1645)		
1 sh., 4to: [–]⁴ / 500 copies	1	
Massachusetts *Laws* (1648)		
17 sh., fol.: A–H⁴, I² / 600 copies	21	
Norris's *Catechism* (1649)		
2 sh., 8vo: A–B⁸ / [800 copies?]	3–4	
Almanacs for 1645–49		
1 sh., 8vo: [5 × 180 copies?]		
Harvard *Theses* and *Quaestiones* for 1645–48		
1½ sheets: [3 × 60 copies?]	2½	
Refuse paper	16	
Paper remaining, May 1649 ("about")	30	
TOTAL	73–4½	74–5½

Per SAMUEL GREEN and HEZEKIAH USHER
Samuel Green and Steven Day, printers

From Dunster account, 1649 (5/0 a ream)		30
Imported by Usher, 1651 (12/0 a ream)		51
Cambridge *Platform* (1649)		
6 sh., 4to:$^{\pi}$A^6 ($\pm$ $^{\pi}$A1.6) A–D^4/		
500 copies	6¼	
Davenport's *Catechism* (1650?)		
[2 sh.?: 800 copies?]	3–4	
Psalms (1651)		
12¼ sh., 16mo in 8's: *^{4}A–V^8, W^8, X–Z^8 / 2000 copies	51	
Massachusetts *Laws*, 1650 Supp. (1651?)		
5 sh., fol.: [500 copies?]	5	
Mather, *Sum of sermons* (1652)		
7½ sh., 4to: $^{\pi}$A^6 A–F^4 / [600 copies?]	9½	
Eliot, *Indian primer* (1653?)		
[3 sh.?: 500 copies?]	3	
Almanacs for 1650–54		
1 sh., 8vo.: [5 × 180 copies?]		
Harvard *Theses* and *Quaestiones*, 1649–51, 53 (2)		
1½ sheets: [5 × 60 copies?]	3	
TOTAL	80–1¾	81

SOURCES:

The Dunster Papers, Harvard University Archives, R.W. Lovett (ed.), "Documents from the Harvard University Archives, 1638–1750," *PCSM* 49 (1975); for the accounts themselves, however, see the more reliable diplomatic transcript of George Parker Winship, *The Cambridge Press* (Philadelphia: Univ. of Penna. Press, 1945), p. 146–7. Winship's pioneering, though hideously digressive discussion of the difficulties of interpretation remains essential, but should be supplemented by the later findings of R.J. Roberts, "A New Cambridge N.E. Imprint: The *Catechisme* of Edward Norris, 1649," *HLB* 13 (1959), 25–8; and Lawrence Granville Starkey, "A Descriptive and Analytical Bibliography of the Cambridge, Massachusetts Press," Univ. of Va. M.A.Thesis, 1949 (published in microform, 1956).

After a number of false starts, Day and Green charge the *Narragansetts*, *Spelling book*, *Capital laws*, *Almanacs*, *Quaestiones* and *Theses* a total of £3–5–0 [= 13 reams] for paper, 1640–49; they estimate the same paper elsewhere in the document separately, at 7 reams (for the first three items) and 5 reams (for the rest)—making a total of only 12. The larger estimate is probably correct, but I have stated the range of possibilities.

There is external evidence for the press runs of the *Narragansetts* (500 copies), the 1654 Supplement to the *Laws* (5–700 copies) and the *Indian primer* (500–1000 copies); Winship, *Cambridge press*, p. 64, 122 and 158. The practise of setting press runs in round figures has encouraged me to correct the stated figure for Mather's *Sum of sermons*, of 9 reams (which would yield about 564 copies) to 9½. There were no graduating classes in 1644, 1648, and 1652 (when Harvard extended the residence required for a B.A. from three to four years). Hence there were no Masters' *Quaestiones* in 1647 and 1651. The general uncertainties in the accounts are within a ream or two, which corresponds well with Day and Green's hesitations and contradictions.

ISBN 0-9764925-5-5

FIRST IMPRESSIONS

Printing in Cambridge, 1639–1989